Are those your
Underpants
on the conveyor?

Are those your Underpants on the conveyor?

Hilarious tales of travel on a very small planet

Mark Sheehan
and friends

NEW
HOLLAND

CONTENTS

PREFACE

Everyone responds to tragedy in their own way.

When President John F. Kennedy was assassinated in 1963, I flicked a hard ball which was autographed by baseball legends Babe Ruth and Mickey Mantle against the wall of our Ohio garage.

I sat there for two days, pummelling that ball as our mother kept us home from school to be near her. Millions of other mothers kept their loved ones home and classrooms across America were empty the week afterwards.

I bounced that ball until the stitching on the seams broke loose, peeled the autographed covering away and kept tossing the ball of twine-like innards.

I kept the skin with the slaughtered signatures for many years in the top of a childhood dresser drawer. A similar ball in pristine condition recently sold at auction for over $8500. My brother David keeps his in a glass cabinet under lock and key.

JFK was my hero, the man who challenged America to put a man on the moon. And bring him home again...
He was my role model and someone I looked up to.

And someone slaughtered him.

I had the same toss-in-the-towel feeling of helplessness after the shocking horror of September Eleven and the cowardly terrorist attacks on America. I didn't feel much like doing anything at all. Again, I felt hopeless. And this time too, I was mourning among millions. My heroes numbered in the thousands, as my own home town of

Manhasset, New York mourned for over 87 breadwinners who would never again catch the 7.22am train from Plandome Station to Penn.

I just kept playing the horrific footage of that second plane, gliding silently into the side of the World Trade Center over and over again with the same cadence that I'd used many years earlier to bounce a ball against a wall. I felt helpless and hopeless for the second time in my life, but only this time it was the smiles and innocent laughter of my children, and my Bridget, who drew me back.

I had loved ones who were counting on me and I again, picked myself up.

On the day our son Cody William was diagnosed, the life expectancy for a cystic fibrosis kid was four to five years of age. My wonderful wife Bridget and I had handed our first-born child a death sentence.

And for the first time ever, I wanted to simply pull the covers over my head, with my family huddled alongside me and never get up again. Ever. Only this time I felt very much alone...

That was over 22 years ago now, and it was the power of my son, and the smiles he held on his face that pushed me from under the covers and made me clear the bedroom threshold. My wife helped me up, and together we were determined to defy all odds with our boy. We made a pact and a promise to each other over our kitchen table in Charleston, South Carolina to do everything we could to keep Cody. Anything.

The power of a small child's laughter, our child's small belly-roll of giggles got me laughing and living again. Cody is my hero now.

Today, there are some very smart people within striking

distance of a cure for cystic fibrosis.

All they need is money now, and I'm hoping that in some small way, this book will reach out and touch others, the way the laugh of a small child reached out and saved me...

This book is dedicated to my son, my Cody, my hero and to all those other CF kids, who plant a foot on the floorboards every day, against some significantly serious odds, and smile...

Laughter is a remarkable healer of the soul. And it can turn corners, see over seemingly insurmountable obstacles and bring complete strangers to heel for each other. I hope you enjoy the medications prescribed in the reading of this small book, and see like I now do the sheer joy to be extracted from a single, genuine laugh.

"Time spent laughing
is time spent with the gods"
—An oriental proverb

1. LANGUAGE BARRIERS

Airport Italian: Anyone?
Nina Mori, JFK International Airport, New York

It was uncommonly quiet at the International Arrivals Building at New York's JFK International Airport—an uncharacteristically civil, unhurried and relaxed atmosphere was probably the result of the off season.

I was working for Alitalia Airlines, and had been assigned to the customs area where I was to assist incoming passengers locate their luggage on the carousel, direct them to the US Customs Agents for baggage inspection and act as interpreter when required.

Without any of the usual frantic calls for assistance, I found myself with little to do on this particular afternoon so I strolled from one customs station to the next, waiting.

At one point, I noticed a small group of well-dressed, middle-aged gentlemen. They were Italian dentists travelling together to attend a seminar in Manhattan. One of these men was standing in front of his open suitcase while an agent slid his hand under a pile of neatly folded shirts and patted the internal compartments of the suitcase before closing it, scribbling something on the customs declaration form and dismissing the man with a casual gesture in the direction of the exit.

The passenger was obviously struggling with his bag— this was before the days of lightweight trolleys on wheels with extractable handles—so I approached him, smiling.

Although I had studied Italian at school, I hadn't had much opportunity to use the language in the real world. I had, however, acquired a good repertoire of airport Italian. I could tell passengers if their flight was on time, direct them to their departure gate or tell them where to pick up duty free items. I had even learned to advise travellers that their flight was delayed for mo-ti-vi-me-te-o-ro-lo-gi-ci—bad weather—and I certainly knew the word for skycap (airline-employed baggage handlers who work for tips.)

"*Posso chiamare un finocchio per lei?* (May I call a skycap for you?)" I offered, imagining he might appreciate assistance with his suitcase. He stared at me with a perplexed expression. I repeated my offer, enunciating as clearly as I could: "*Un finocchio. Per la sua valigia. Sembra pesante.*" (A skycap. For your suitcase. It looks heavy.)

Still, not a word of response, just a puzzled expression: not hostile, but not friendly either.

I repeated the question in a tone and expression that I hoped transmitted my annoyance: "*Signore. Un finocchio. Per portare la sua valigia. Cos'è che non capisce?* (Sir. A skycap. To carry your suitcase. What is it that you don't understand?)"

Suddenly, a small light went off in my head. Somewhere in my brain, a thought was trying to materialise, to push its way to the surface. I excused myself and hurried over to a Italian-speaking colleague who was wandering around nearby.

"Gianni, what's the work for 'skycap' in Italian?" I asked, already beginning to realise my mistake but hoping against hope I was wrong.

"Facchino," he answered. "Why?"

"Oh, shit," I muttered as I turned around and went back to where my little dentist was watching me suspiciously, head cocked to one side, eyes narrowed. My face was hot and, no doubt, very red.

"*Volevo dire facchino?* (Can I offer you a skycap?)," I said, with great emphasis on the correct word for skycap. As I apologised for my mistake, I saw his face soften and the corners of his mouth turn upward.

He broke into a full-fledged smile, shook his head from side to side and turned toward the exit. As he walked away, I saw his shoulders rise and fall in what I'm sure was quiet laughter.

I don't know if it was his first trip to the United States, but I'm quite sure it was the first time he had been offered the services of a homosexual by a slang-talking airport worker—as soon as he stepped off the plane in a foreign land! Thanks for that, Gianni!

Hotel California Happy Hour
Mark Sheehan, Amsterdam

"Americans who travel abroad for the first time are often shocked to discover that, despite all the progress that has been made in the last 30 years, many foreign people still speak in foreign languages"
—Dave Barry

TrekAmerica was a travel company I worked for, designed for young people to discover the states. I should have known better when the entire team of eight TrekAmerica sales gurus greeted me at the curbside in Amsterdam, smiling broadly and telling me that I had nailed a perfect park. When I pointed out the fact that I was about a half-mile from the curb and sticking out into rush hour traffic, my peers simply attached themselves to the fenders and bounced my rental car sideways to the curb.

It was a Friday afternoon, and the Trek troops were already an hour late in enjoying the hotel's 4pm happy hour. I discovered how little this mattered as happy hour was extended to 4am the next morning.

The California Hotel was dead-centre in the red light district of Amsterdam and my 'mates' had done enough window shopping for the day, and they were eager to get on the grog. My escorts whisked away my bags, registered me and got my room key.

They'd planned a literary surprise in my honour and ushered me straight into the hotel's living room-like bar to meet "Harry", the bar-keep. Harry had apparently helped kill the brain cells of such literary greats as Ernest Hemingway, Tennessee Williams, Ford Madox Ford, James Jones and Hunter S. Thompson.

It was a set-up to get me sauteed and slaughtered from the very start.

My not-so-well-kept bar-keep launched himself across the varnished bar-top, cameras came from nowhere, light flashes and temporarily blinded us. I was encouraged to ring the bar's brass bell, in the same way, I was told, other great writers had done before me.

With the encouragement of my mates, I rang the bell loudly, proudly and frequently. What I did not fully appreciate until the Monday morning check-out was that the tradition of 'ringing the bell' meant that every drink across the bar, for friend or foe, was 'on the house' and to be put on the tab of the well-lubricated bell-ringer.

The cost of beds for our entire sales crew was a whopping eight dollars per head a night including the continental breakfast. The bar bill for my bell-ringing activities was well over $900. When I asked what my peers had put into the pot for the bar bill and our bedsprings, I was advised that each of them had slithered out early and were Gone, Gone, Gone!

Two days later and significantly 'slung-over' I paid a whopping big $300 fine, and towing charges for having parked across an elderly veteran and disabled neighbour's driveway, within full view of HUGE HANDICAPPED, 24-hour No-Parking-under-penalty-of-death sign in Dutch. The handsome signage when translated later, proclaimed: "Don't Even Dream of Parking Here—You Idiot! Ever!

The attending officer who handed over the papers for the release of my lease car was draped in a neck-to-ankle Gestapo jacket, an automatic Israeli-built Uzi strapped across his back. He looked at me like unsightly bathtub scum.

When he handed over the keys, he asked how long I was intending on staying in Holland. Bastards!

Wind Break
Trevor Lake
Silk Road, China

I was leading a group of tourists down the Silk Road in China and our primary goal was to see if we could find the last remnants of the Great Wall. So, every time I saw a pile of bricks, I would ask my Chinese guide if it was the Great Wall.

One afternoon I saw the usual pile of bricks and asked the guide what it was. He knew but could not think of the English words. He explained that it was a shield stone the locals used to hide behind when the desert winds got too strong. I explained to him that it was what we call a 'windbreak'. He dutifully noted the word and meaning in his notebook.

The following day we were all standing atop a large sand dune in the Gobi Desert and the winds were gusting, threatening to blow away one of the lady's sun hats. My guide, keen to try out his new words, stood next to her and proudly said: "Would you like me to stand next to you and break wind?"

The Blind Leading the Dumb
Shane, Cabo San Lucas, Mexico

This is a true story told to me by my friend Shane

Shane was determined to learn Spanish and had recruited another long-haul travel companion, Jack Benson, to coach him along. Jack had been studying Spanish for months in readiness for the trip, from his frost-smitten home town of Minneapolis, Minnesota—a town where, in winter, you're forced to learn another language, build an ark in the living room, carve duck decoys or learn how to produce pipe bombs from scratch. Anything to avoid going anywhere near the outdoors.

Jack possessed a dog-eared pocket dictionary of Spanish he bought for 50 cents at Saint Vincent de Paul and was intent on using it to enlighten, inspire and educate Shane to master some functional Mexican.

Being a real stickler for pronunciation, Jack insisted that Shane practise in front of the mirror during lessons.

One of the first questions every good traveller needs to get under their belt early on is how to find the toilet in a timely manner. Jack was going to teach Shane how to ask where the bathroom was located, please.

Jack also advised Shane that in matters of Mexican culture any query about toilet-location questions must never, ever be addressed to a female. It might be taken as a massive insult by the woman's family and could incur serious cultural consequences. The Mexicans are well known for protecting their women—it's called "Machismo".

With about four hours of practice, Shane had his "where-can-I-take-a-pee, please" Spanish nailed down to perfection. He could roll the sentence off his tongue with the sleekness of a fully-suited Mexican matador.

In the first bar we encountered in Mexico, Shane proudly approached the enormous male bar-keep, who was sporting a stereotypical, yet extremely intimidating handlebar moustache.

Shane cleared his throat and confidently asked: "*Qantos pesos por su hermana*?" Properly translated, this question actually meant, "How many pesos for your sister?"

Buzzed by the Bus!
Jeff Zack, Jerusalem

After high school, I spent my first year of college studying and working in Israel. The first half of the year I studied at Hebrew University in Jerusalem, where among other subjects I learned just enough Hebrew to get by around town. Or at least I thought it was enough to get around.

The second half of the year was spent working at a popcorn packaging plan on a kibbutz in the south of Israel. One weekend, I planned to leave the kibbutz to spend time with friends back in Jerusalem.

A shared cab took me from the kibbutz to the entrance of the city, where I then planned to take the 23 bus to the University. While I waited for the 23, I noted that the bus stop had a sign which listed over a dozen different busses that would stop there. There were so many listed that no destinations or other information was listed—just bus route numbers. Fortunately, the 23 was listed on the sign.

After some time, the 23 still had not arrived, and I started noticing the same bus numbers coming and going. At one point I counted the same bus number arrive five different times!

As my wait time approached an hour, I started to doubt whether I was indeed waiting in the right place. Jerusalem's Central Bus Station, where all buses passed through, was only a short walk away, but I kept thinking that the moment I gave up on this spot and went to the bus station, my bus would arrive. So I waited, frustrated and tired.

Finally, after an interminable wait, the 23 arrived. As I walked (alone) up to the front doors, the middle doors opened and a number of people walked off. But the front doors did not open. Having learned the value of being assertive in this country, I knocked on the doors and looked at the bus driver, who stared ahead and ignored me. I banged louder.

Finally, the doors opened and the bus driver started yelling at me in Hebrew. This is a loose translation of what I thought was said:

Driver: "What do you want?"

Me: "To go to Hebrew University."

Driver: "What do you want?"

Me: (Louder, thinking he hadn't heard): "TO GO TO HEBREW UNIVERSITY!"

Driver: "This isn't the right bus."

Me: (Thinking he's pulling my leg) "Yes it is!"

Driver: (Getting angry) "This isn't the right bus! Look at the sign!"

Me: (Getting angry too) "Look at the sign? Why don't you look?! 23! It's right there! Let me on!"

Now, in retrospect I realise he must have said some other things, including that this was the last stop for the 23 and that you could only board at the Central Bus Station. But at the time, I only understood his rude attitude, the slamming doors in my face and the sense his refusal to let me board was a prank or some other joke that I clearly did not get.

Angry, I did what any teenager would do: I flipped the driver the bird and swore.

The driver slammed on the brakes and the bus screeched to a halt. Immediately regretting my actions, I started to back away as the bus doors opened, and the huge driver clambered down the stairs, run at me, and got right in my face.

I'd broken the "English barrier", so to speak:

Driver: "F**k you? You want me to f**k you? I'll f**k you!"

At that point, the driver reared back, clenched his fist and started to follow through at my face. I had a split second to make one of two choices: duck, saving my face but possibly angering him further, or stand there and hope he'd be satisfied with a single punch.

I closed my eyes, braced myself and waited for the impact.

After a few seconds had passed, and I felt nothing, I opened my eyes. The driver's closed fist was millimetres from my nose, just hanging there in mid-air. We stared at each other awkwardly for a few moments, his fist still lingering.

Sensing an opportunity, I turned and began slowly walking away, headed to the bus station. I didn't want to run, fearing he'd chase me, but instead hoped that calmly walking away would diffuse the situation.

As I made my way down the hill, I felt more and more relieved as I failed to sense any lumbering form running in my direction. Then, rather than a person, I felt something much bigger coming towards me, and fast. I turned and saw the driver, in his bus, hurtling down the street in my direction.

At first I assumed he would just buzz by me in an attempt to scare me. I was wrong. As the bus approached, gaining speed, the driver slid closer and closer to the curb—and then, to my surprise, jumped the curb and continued in my direction, driving half on the sidewalk and half on the street!

This time I decided that staying put and waiting for impact was unwise. Luckily there were bushes next to the sidewalk and, as the bus whizzed passed, I quickly dove into one of them. The bus passed, slid back onto the street and then disappeared into the distance.

I stood up, brushed myself off, collected my backpack and headed down the hill to the bus station.

Clearly my Hebrew still had substantial room for improvement!

Speaking with a Forked Tongue
Mark Sheehan, America from coast to coast

The Lone Ranger and Tonto went camping in the desert. After they got their tent all set up, both men fell sound asleep. Some hours later, Tonto wakes the Lone Ranger and says, "Kemo Sabe, look towards sky, what you see?"

The Lone Ranger replies, "I see millions of stars."

"What that tell you?'" asks Tonto.

The Lone Ranger ponders for a minute then says, "Astronomically speaking, it tells me there are millions of galaxies and potentially billions of planets. Astrologically,

it tells me that Saturn is in Leo. Time wise, it appears to be approximately a quarter past three in the morning.
Theologically, the Lord is all-powerful and we are small and insignificant. Meteorologically, it seems we will have a beautiful day tomorrow.
What's it tell you, Tonto?"
"You dumber than buffalo shit," Tonto says. "It means someone stole the tent."

I was guiding a group of young tourists with TrekAmerica, across America, and they were constantly berating American beer.

They'd rant and rave about how piss-weak American lager was and the fact that it had no octane compared to the good grog they enjoyed at home. Being a proud American, I quietly took offence, even if our lager was a bit light-on. It might have been a lot better to swallow the truth if a fellow American said it.

By the time we hit New Orleans and the French Quarter, I'd had enough of their brew belly-aching. It was time to retaliate. I marched the entire troop onto Bourbon Street in the French Quarter, and used the food kitty to buy everyone a massive plastic cupful of Hurricane Cocktail. As we walked around town I said, "When in Rome, do as the Romans do", and enlightened them on jazz, the famous Mardi Gras and other tidbits of local colour.

A Hurricane Cocktail is made of four or five different types of booze, and is mixed in with something that makes the entire concoction taste like soda pop or Hawaiian Punch.

Naturally, my Trekkers loudly boasted it was yet another American sissy drink.

So I reloaded their tumblers for another tasting. We

strolled Bourbon Street in 90°F of heat and humidity until the fire-water concoction kicked in. By then these tougher-than-shoe-leather liquor Dons were drooling out of the side of their mouths, speaking in forked tongues and slurring their words with newly acquired southern accents.

The locals are fond of saying about a well-constructed Hurricane Cocktail that: "Two of dem is one too many!"

We still don't know to this day how my West Australian farmer wound up in the water fountain of Louie Armstrong Park.

At six the next morning I banged a huge cook pot with a steel spoon to roust my Trekkers. They screamed in painful degrees of duress for me to stop. I distributed aspirins over coffee to everyone and never heard a bad word again about American drinking habits.

Nine months after that fateful encounter with the Hurricane Cocktail, Kerrie from Canberra gave birth to an eight-pound boy. She married one of the TrekAmerica leaders about four months after giving birth and I think they're still together. I wonder if they called their baby Hurricane?

2. AIRLINE WOES AND PROS

"When you're travelling, you are what you are right there and then. People don't have your past to hold against you. There are no yesterdays on the road."
—William Least Heat Moon (From Blue Highways)

According to some very reliable statistics, shopping has been the number one activity enjoyed by overseas visitors to the United States. And on every tour I've ever run, we always allow the last day for a shopping spree, so our happy customers could tote home things they didn't want to drag around the countryside for weeks beforehand. In the early years, items like running shoes, blue jeans, linens, booze and jewellery topped the lists.

Nowadays things have escalated to the extreme with our friends from overseas buying small tractors, water blasters, golf carts and the occasional Ford Mustang!

Left the Batteries In
Jesse Brain
America

Jessie Brain is often a guest at our dinner table and I loved this story she told about a shopping outing she went on in America with her mother

For my twenty-first birthday my mother and I went on a holiday across America, visiting Los Angeles, Las Vegas and New York. We had an amazing trip with plenty of laughs. We wanted to take something back home in the form of some goofy gifts for our friends.

My mother bought a dozen mini punching bags that shouted expletives when punched.

When the stern-faced American security officials picked up our bags and threw them onto the conveyor belt to be screened, twelve little voices yelled out phrases such as 'Eat shit', "Lick my bum!", 'F**k you' and 'Dirt bag!'. She forgot to take the batteries out!

If only I had a camera to take a photo of their faces,

although I'm sure that would have got my mother and I into even more trouble.

Tales of a Travel Agent

Travel agents often get unusual requests from consumers, and our Italian contact, Piero has posted a fair few doozies

I once had someone ask for an aisle seat on a flight so their hair wouldn't get messy being near the window.

Another client called in inquiring about a package to Hawaii. After going over all the cost info, she asked, "Would it be cheaper to fly to California then take the train to Hawaii?"

I got a call from a woman who wanted to go to Cape Town. I started to explain the length of the flight and the passport information when she interrupted me with, "I'm not trying to make you look stupid, but Cape Town is in Massachusetts." Without trying to make her look like the stupid one, I calmly explained, "Cape Cod is in Massachusetts, Cape Town is in Africa." Her response... click...she hung up on me.

A man once called, furious about a Florida package we did for him. I asked what was wrong with the vacation in Orlando. He said he was expecting an ocean-view room. I tried to explain that is not possible, since Orlando is in the middle of the state. He replied, "Don't lie to me. I looked on the map and Florida is a very thin state."

I got a call from a gentleman who asked, "Is it possible to see England from Canada?" I said, "No." He said, "But they look so close on the map."

Another man called and asked if he could rent a car in Dallas. I pulled up the reservation and noticed he had a one-hour lay-over in Dallas. When I asked him why he wanted to rent a car, he said, "I heard Dallas was a big airport, and I need a car to drive between the gates to save time."

A nice lady called one day. She needed to know how it was possible that her flight from Detroit left at 8.20am and got into Chicago, about 380km (236 miles) by air away, at 8.33am. I tried to explain that the state of Michigan, where Detroit is, was an hour ahead of Illinois, where Chicago is, but she just could not understand the concept of time zones. Finally I told her the plane went very fast, and she bought that!

A woman called our offices a few years back and asked, "Do airlines put your physical description on your bag so they know whose luggage belongs to who?" I said, "No, why do you ask?" She replied, "Well, when I checked in with the airline, they put a tag on my luggage that said FAT, and I'm overweight—is there any connection?" After putting her on hold for a minute while I "looked into it" (I was actually laughing) I came back and explained the city code for Fresno, California is FAT, and that the airline was just putting a destination tag on her luggage.

I once got off the phone with a man who asked, "How do I know which plane to get on?" I asked him what exactly he meant, and he replied, "I was told my flight number is 823, but none of these darn planes have numbers on them.

On another occasion, a woman said, "I need to fly to Pepsi-Cola on one of those computer planes." I asked if she meant to fly to Pensacola in Florida on a commuter plane. She said, "Yeah, whatever."

Then there was the time a businessman called and had a

question about the documents he needed in order to fly to China. After a lengthy discussion about passports, I reminded him he needed a visa. "Oh no, I don't, I've been to China many times and never had to have one of those." I double checked and sure enough, his stay required a visa. When I told him this he said, "Look, I've been to China four times and every time they have accepted my American Express."

I heard about a woman who called to make reservations and said, "I want to go from Chicago to Hippopotamus, New York." The agent was at a loss for words. Finally, the agent said, "Are you sure that's the name of the town?" "Yes, what flights do you have?" replied the customer.

After some searching, the agent came back with, "I'm sorry, ma'am, I've looked up every airport code in the country and can't find a Hippopotamus anywhere." The customer retorted, "Oh don't be silly. Everyone knows where it is. Check your map!" The agent scoured a map of the state of New York and finally offered, "You don't mean Buffalo, do you?" "That's it!" she said. "I knew it was a big animal!"

Neither Here Nor There
Andrea Black, SkyMall via iPod

I was six years old when I reclined on my first economy seat. It was a Qantas flight to Heathrow, via Bombay (now Mumbai) in India. The colour scheme was orange and red. I remember my mum complained about the steak (too tough) and an air hostess made me laugh when she placed a serviette under my sleeping dad's dribble-laden chin.

I also remember feeling in a state I had never felt

before. I was neither here nor there, in what's known as a luminal place, and it was pure bliss. They say half the fun is getting there. I'd push it to two-thirds, after all, it's the journey not the destination that counts.

Thirty years and many flight miles later and I'm settling down: leafing through my SkyMall™ catalogue—the magazine equivalent of late-night infomercials—on a flight from Los Angeles. In my excited limbo-like state of mind, everything in the magazine looks appealing. They know that no-one on the ground could possibly want or need a "poop freeze", described as a spray refrigerant that "chills animal turds to -62°F, creating an outer "crust" that enables you to quickly pick up poop and place in a bag." Yet in the air, it's a great idea! Why I'll order one for my friend Melanie as well!

I'm listening to a mix on my iPod when I get a tap on the shoulder from the man in the next seat. 'Am I on there?' He asks, pointing to my music device. He looks familiar but I can't quite place him. I laugh and say, "Maybe you are, there's a lot of music on here." He tries to help me identify him by singing a chorus in my ear. Immediately I recognise it, a huge hit in the early 1990s, but I still can't remember his name and feel embarrassed to ask.

We clink glasses and small talk about my musical taste (it's old soul, mostly), his taste (Jamaican dub) and his upcoming shows. His name still eludes me and it's driving me mad. But I can't ask him because he thinks I know.

Finally, a chance! He excuses himself to visit the bathroom and I lean over and look for a bag-tag, a laminate, anything that might give me a clue. Nothing.

He comes back and we continue our conversation, a couple of music lovers hovering above the Pacific. Soon we're singing harmonies to Sam Cooke gospel songs before he went secular.

Plane travel has been described as solitude without isolation. We all have a common goal, to get there, and a certain camaraderie can build between seat mates that might not happen on the ground. For a few hours it felt like me and what's-his-name were best friends. He showed me pictures of his wife and kids, I played him songs by my husband's band. We toasted together.

Another toilet break from him. I am not sure if it was the thin air, but I threw caution to the wind and went into his bag, actually rifled. This daring feat wouldn't and couldn't be done on the ground, yet here I was, invincible. There are no rules. After all, we are in what ethnologist Marc Auge calls a "non-place".

And just as I opened his wallet and clumsily pulled out an ID card which revealed the name, I noticed a determined air steward approaching me. Sprung! Would I be handcuffed, the plane forced to land at the nearest terminal? How could I explain to my new friend that I wasn't trying to steal his cash. I just wanted to verify his name?

The flight crew member sidled up to me and said, in a hushed tone, "Excuse me, ma'am, but is this man bothering you? If he is, I can have him moved." Him bothering me? I was the one going through his personal belongings, I'm the nuisance here! I assured her I was quite fine thank you very much. Didn't she know who he was?

My new bestie came back to his seat and I smiled and hummed his hit, we embraced as we disembarked and said our goodbyes. Amazingly, I saw him at another airport a few years later. He didn't recognise me but this time I knew exactly who he was, but I wasn't going to say hello. Real life is different from when you're up in the air.

Throw Down the Firestones!
John Cachia, RAAF Hercules

John is one of the founding-board members of the Jellyfish Club, a loosely-packed crew of folks who have survived the tourism and travel trade.

Ansett Airlines used to run flights in competition to Qantas in Australia. During the national pilots' dispute in March 1989, no aircraft from any airline were being flown by local pilots.

Ansett and Qantas both 'wet leased' a number of aircraft from carriers around the world to keep up with demand. For example, if you looked along the domestic terminal you would see the following livery on the tarmac: South West Airlines from the US, Croatia Airlines and Royal Brunei, the personal airline of the Sultan of Brunei.

One day I was driving to work when overhead, coming in to land, were a couple of RAAFC-130 Hercules. Not only are these buggers HUGE, but they are incredibly noisy! Yes, as you guessed it, we were using Royal Australian Air Force aircraft to fly passengers around the network!

What added to my amusement were the businessmen and women, in their suits and skirts sitting in the belly of the Hercules strapped in and wearing earmuffs.

Of course the Hercules didn't have cabin service, so we provided the passengers with a little container of refreshments. To add to the adventure, the Hercules is a big and slow moving aircraft, and so where a jet would take an hour to get to Melbourne, the Hercules would take 2½ hours!

Once the aircraft landed and taxied to its parking bay, the tail of the Hercules would drop open and out would trundle the 'commercial passengers' somewhat dishevelled and cramped, hearing a buzz in their ears... A quick clean of the aircraft and it was ready for boarding again, earmuffs and all!

"Never travel with anyone you care about. You blame each other for everything that goes wrong..."
—T. S. Elliot

Unclaimed Baggage
Martin Korn, Business class to Hong Kong

In the late summer of 1984 my ex-wife and I were returning to our home in Hong Kong from a rather unpleasant trip back to Germany. Our marriage was slowly turning towards disaster.

In Frankfurt, Germany we boarded Cathay Pacific flight CX288—forever my favourite flight number. In those days this wasn't a non-stop service to Hong Kong as the 747-200s needed a refuelling stop in Dubai.

We had business class tickets and were seated in the first row just below the movie screen. We found our seats and my wife gave me a hard time with some on-board storage chores she wanted me to do. I reluctantly obliged. I was standing there, looking back over the enclosed business class section to see if there was a more friendly or familiar face on board. There was nobody I knew. But my eagle eye spotted right away one single Asian lady—a beauty, hot, exactly my type...what can I say?

I thought, "Why is it that I can never be seated next to something like that?" Instead I had my wife next to me and giving me a hard time.

But it was obviously my lucky day. The traveller to the

other side of me wanted to be relocated so he could sit next to his wife and that was exactly this beauty's seat. So— alas—the beauty was moved right next to me and the other frequent flyer was happily seated alongside his wife.

Now I had to manage a very delicate approach to not make my soon-to-be-ex-wife explode in front of all the other passengers. She is Italian and part of our problems stemmed from her fiery temperament.

I introduced myself to the beauty and found out she was actually a flight attendant with that same airline and also returning from a European vacation. Was she alone? Of course not—duh! So where is the boyfriend? She explained to me that her man was also German, but he was sitting in first class! Wow, I thought, that is some dude, letting this beautiful bird roam alone in business while he sat in 1A.

And as coincidence had it, the guy was even working for the competitor of my company in Germany. He was the representative for them in Korea, whereas I was the representative stationed in Hong Kong for all Asia. Small world.

The beauty also had a name—Inja. She told me to think of Ninja without the N in front. Now that was unforgettable. I introduced her—reluctantly—to my wife. It is interesting to observe how women smell immediately the scent of competition. A very frosty hello was exchanged. So here I am, sitting between Mrs Iceberg to my left and Miss Happy and, yes, flirty to my right.

The first half of the flight was during daytime, with the sumptuous lunch, drinks and lots of small talk to my right side.

When we arrived in Dubai, the doors opened and everything was very busy. Passengers were all up and shaking out their legs and getting ready for the next leg of the flight to Hong Kong. Inja wanted to introduce me to my countryman, Mr First Class.

A good little while on the ground passed until the first class man showed up in our lower business class quarters. He had a moustache, wore brass rimmed glasses and had the habit of looking over your head.

So here is Inja, with her very lively, open and super friendly way to introduce us and make a joke of how funny it is that he works for that company and I for that other one.

She introduces us, I extend my hand to him and he doesn't take it! He refuses to shake my hand! I can't believe it. Frankly, I'm still shocked today that such a thing is even possible. It was the only time in my life that someone has refused to take my extended hand for a handshake.

Now that didn't go down well at all, as you might imagine. Yes, I'm honest—I swore revenge. I had nothing really to say to him at that point, which cut the conversation short. The interesting part was that he hadn't anything much to say to his girlfriend either. So after a short and rather negative little visit in the lower business class quarters he disappeared back to where he thought he belonged—first class.

The flight took off again towards the Orient. After the embarrassing show of her boyfriend, our bond grew closer. The on board movie was *Romancing The Stone* with Michael Douglas and Katherine Turner. We had a blast together—giggling, laughing and making funny comments. It felt as if we were a couple. But no monkey business. To my left, my frosty other half was sleeping through...or pretending to sleep through.

When we arrived, both couples were fighting at the

baggage belt. We must have been at the same crossroads. I met Inja again months later at a New Year's Eve party of a common friend. We immediately clicked again and...the rest is history.

The moral of this little tale? If you want to hold on to your precious belongings do not upgrade yourself and leave the rest behind.

Believe it or Not
John Cachia, Golden West Airlines

A friend of mine, who we will call Captain Klutz, worked for Golden West Airlines for 20 years. The airline is now defunct, but for many years it was based in Los Angeles. He told me some hilarious air travel stories.

The "Marvin Mainliner" pilots from United were always joking with us about our fleet. Once they had said to us in the airport on our way out, "Do you wear a bag over your heads when you fly that shoebox, because you're so embarrassed?" They were referring to our Shorts 33, a turboprop commuter airplane we regularly flew.

Once, when we were taxiing out to the runway in a Shorts 33, our pilots grabbed some lunch bags, cut out some holes and put them over their heads, waving to United's B747 crew as it taxied by their gate for takeoff. One of the airline's stock-holders witnessed this from his vantage point in the terminal and decided to complain. The chief pilot's office then issued a new flight rule: "PILOTS WILL NOT FLY WITH BAGS OVER THEIR HEADS!"

Checking In...or Not?
Bill Bryson, America

The wonderful and downright "out there" writer penned a series of columns for Night and Day magazine many years ago. In one of Bill's columns, he described the agonies of trying to board an airplane without photo ID. In the end, he was at the mercy of an airline official who, after looking at the author's photograph on the back of the book jacket of his best-selling travel book, allowed him to board

The well-dressed and pompous fellow at the airline ticket counter was irritating everyone else who was stuck in the same delayed-for-hours flight situation. His snide comments, broadcasted to the young gal at the ticket counter, were delivered loudly enough so that everyone in the lounge knew this VIP was going to make a massive stink about the delay.

The gal behind the check-in desk was trying hard to remain calm with a crowd that had begun to take on the shape of a lynching party. The chap strode to the desk and said, "How can this be possible! Do you HAVE ANY IDEA WHO I AM?!"—at which point the young gal took up the microphone and asked the frustrated travellers, with great calm and curiosity, "The gentlemen at the desk alongside me appears to have forgotten who he is. Can anyone here help him?"

The mounting revolt broke in uncontrolled laughter and the situation was defused. The pouting VIP picked up his expensive leather attaché case and stormed off in search of a higher authority, insisting on the girl's full first name.

Sometimes you just need to see things from a different point of view.

Pilot Poos and Plots

An airline pilot finishes talking to the passengers after the plane has taken off, and forgets to turn off the intercom. He says to the co-pilot, "I think I'll go take a dump and then put the make on that new blonde stewardess." The stewardess hears it and runs up the aisle to tell him the intercom is still on. She trips and falls in her haste. A little old lady looks down at her and says, "There's no rush, honey. He said he had to take a dump first."

Potty-Training at 35,000 Feet
Cheryl Anderson, on board a plane

OK, this one is really going to be hard to believe. A first-class passenger was in the lavatory for 20 minutes and the stewardess asked his wife if she thought he was OK or perhaps needed assistance.

The wife suggested that his "movements" just take him a while longer to accomplish these days. A few minutes later the 'Help Light' in the toilet went on, signaling a potential emergency situation.

The stewardess opened the door, thinking the man might be in serious trouble.

But there he was, sitting on the pot with pants nested down around his ankles and saying: "Dear, I'm going to be in here for a while. I have really bad diarrhoea. Could you bring me a Scotch on the rocks, please?"

3. TRAINS MOVING ON DOWN THE LINE

*"When a man is wrapped up in himself,
it makes a very small package..."*
–John Ruskin, English journalist

Try Doing Your Nails When You're on the Rails!

Mark Sheehan, Boston

I took the train from Washington DC to Boston to visit a fast-lane and slightly older lass I'd met at a publishing convention. She was the editor of a very porn-oriented magazine published by *Hustler*'s wheelchair-bound Larry Flynt.

I liked the girl because she had great curb-side and bed-side appeal. The evening parties at the convention she toted me along to were much better than the ones I was meant to be attending with *Organic Gardening, Popular Mechanics* and *Healthy Life* magazines. We had a great weekend in Washington DC.

So when I dragged my somewhat exhausted ass to its assigned Amtrak seat on the night train back home, I was assailed by the strong vapour of fingernail polish. It was being applied to some fantastic fingers. The fingers were attached to a stunning brunette, smiling at me. She hoped I'd be OK with her vapours.

I thought I must have done something good in another life to have this magnificent creature to keep me company.

We hit it off instantly, lubricated by four or five swift visits to the bar car for liquid refreshments—and like one of those letters to the editor of *Penthouse* or *Playboy*, this lass opened up to me in ways I'd never dreamed possible in public. Mind you, it was a red-eye night train, but even with the cabin lighting dimmed we managed to find places and positions I'd previously only read about.

In the Boston terminal, she reluctantly gave me her phone number—and before jumping into a cab, I called her, wanting her to arrive home and hear my voice on her answering machine.

"Sorry, the number you're trying to reach is incorrect, or no longer in service. If you think you've reached this number in error, please check the number and try again later..."

When I turned to find her in the crowd, she was gone. It appears she purchased a one-way ticket. Whenever I have the option now, I always opt for the night train.

Sleeping Car—Take the Train
Tom Kennedy, Long Island

After one overly playful St. Patrick's Day in New York City, I boarded the Long Island railroad with a carriage full of other well-lubricated revellers, all of whom claimed to be Irish. It was a no-smoking carriage, which was a good thing because the alcohol levels in the airstream might have ignited with all the high octane fumes in the carriage space.

The clack-clack of the tracks soon put our merry band into a slumber, and like my friends in various stages of green dress (or undress) I slept sweetly, until the train hit the last station on the line. A good 20 miles or more beyond our home-front stations.

It was the last train of the evening, and the conductors simply left us snoring sweetly and sleeping in the darkened cars, until morning when commuters in pin-striped suits and copies of the *Wall Street Journal* boarded at breakfast.

Snow Blind and Cold Cops
Paul Campbell, Plandome, Long Island

Paul Campbell taught himself to drive his older sisters' VW Beatle long before he could see over the windshield, and I used to be impressed when he'd rock up at our house by car in the 8th grade. He put the Yellow Pages™ under his ass, and had wooden pegs he used to lift the level of the pedals for his feet.

In those days, Plandome was a sanctuary of private estates and famous folks and our parents paid for our own police and fire departments. Which meant the Plandome Police tended to turn a blind eye to Paul's practices behind the wheel. Paul's' dad ran Hearst Publishing and paid big, really big, taxes.

One snowy evening, I and my crew did a little car cruise out on Long Island, and somewhere near Huntington we stopped to roll a few joints. There were four of us in a VW bug, enjoying a couple of doobies, and the eight-track was blaring the Grateful Dead at high decibels. Because it was snowing we kept the windows rolled up, and pleasant smoke filled the tiny car like a scene from a Cheech and Chong movie about getting high in high school.

I pulled into a big vacant parking lot and stopped to enjoy my share...when out of nowhere a Nassau County patrol car pulled up. I quickly got out and approached the officer's car so he wouldn't get a contact high if he came to the VW's car door.

The officer sat snuggly behind the wheel, his heater on full bore, and I passed my licence and registration through the window. I was respectful, something my parents drilled into me, calling him "Sir" and smiling widely. He was warm and seated, and I was submissively standing in the cold with my jacket open. And looking back on the event, I was also very stoned.

When he handed me back my papers, he said he'd just stopped to be sure we were OK, rolled the window up and was gone as swiftly as he'd arrived.

When I looked back at the VW I couldn't even see inside because the thick smoke from the joints had fully fogged-up the windows.

Pouring out of a small breach in the passenger window was a vapour trail of pot smoke that resembled a Christmas chimney. When I asked my high-as-a-kite-crew why they continued to light up the dope, right under the nose of the cop, they said they'd been completely unaware the cop was even on the scene. They thought I'd simply stepped away from the car to take a pee.

After my heart had resumed its normal beat, we drove on...

Riding the Rails
Mark Sheehan, Long Island

Growing up on Long Island meant that riding the railroad for free became an obsession for me. Perhaps the worst and most chronic of my earlier addictions was to see if I could chalk up more free rides on the Long Island Railroad than any of my equally acne-covered buddies.

In the process of looking for a 'free ride', I created a way of riding the rails. Railway stations along Long Island at that time had two different platform levels, which required the carriage builders to adapt to customers walking straight onto and off the train, or descending four steps to reach the ground. So the train carriage manufacturers created a clever steel grid on hinges, with a handrail which could be lifted or dropped depending on the height of the station.

When closed, this provided a little under-the-train- cave which could handsomely hide two idiot kids. The handrail, which normally aided commuters going up and down, helped idiots like me to hold on and stay inside the stairwell when the train was tearing across the tracks and trestles. Because the train only ever used one side of the carriage to exit station platforms, we had the entire unused side of the carriages as duel kid nests in-between stations.

On some evenings, there would be as many as 24 stupid asses like myself, packed in pairs into the stairwells and joy-riding up and down Long Island in the dark. When the train pulled into a station, we would simply, discreetly, slip out of our hiding places, avoiding the deadly electrical third rail, hug the side of the carriage to avoid detection and then crawl in underneath the station platform and wait for a train headed in the other direction.

Each station garnered another notch in our bragging rights. Some of us kept detailed log books, like pilots do with each flight. This was long before black boxes were introduced.

And if my kids ever did anything like that, I'd whoop 'em good.

4. AUTOMOBILE ANECDOTES: THE WHEEL-DEAL!

I've had a love affair with the open road for as long as I could pour milk on my own cereal. The lure of the open road still can distract me from taking out the garbage, doing the dishes or cleaning out the garage. If you need anything at all from the shops, I've already got the keys gingerly jingling in my palm. If it has got a motor under it, I'm gone!

"When you come to a fork in the road...take it"
—Legendary baseball figure Yogi Berra

Who turned the kettle off?

In 2000, Merv Grazinski of Oklahoma City purchased a brand new Winnebago motor-home. On the maiden voyage, Merv set the cruise control according to the owner's manual at a cool 100 kilometres (60 miles) per hour and calmly retired from the driver's seat to go into the galley and whip himself up a pot of coffee.

Not surprisingly the vehicle left the freeway, crashed and overturned a few times.

Grazinski sued Winnebago for false advertising and the jury awarded him $1,750,000 plus a new Winnebago motor-home to go along with the cash.

Who'd figure? When ole Merv bought the first, ill-fated vehicle, the owner's manual never actually SAID you had to stay behind the wheel and steer with the cruise control on. It does now.

Making a Pit Stop on the Bus
Bill Dosset (Mimi Goodyear's hubby), New Orleans

I was in Mexico with a summer program conducted by Tulane University in New Orleans. This guy seated next to me a bus looked up and panicked, thinking the bus driver had skipped his stop.

He started yelling to the bus driver in what was Spanish for, "Please stop, you missed my stop." After several times in Spanish, he jumped up and yelled in English, "Stop the bus, You Idiot!"

The bus driver screeched to a stop and shook his fist at the student, who shook his fist back at the bus driver. The driver suddenly pulled over and opened the door as commanded. The equally angry passenger grumbled as he stomped off the bus and out the door and fell into an open manhole, where he promptly disappeared.

The odd bit about it was the driver had not missed his stop. It was another half block up the road.

On the Bus with The Beatles

In 1964, my fourth grade class took a field trip to The Henry Ford Museum in Dearborn, Michigan, the home of the Ford motor company

It was almost like a trip to Disneyland, only we didn't have our parents along for the ride.

The adventure was my first of many road trips in a real motor coach, equipped with a toilet at the back, curtains on the windows and a microphone at the front for the teachers to yell at us with. My seat back tilted and I had a little overhead net to keep my mother's paper-bag lunch goodies out of harm's way.

I sat next to my best friend Jerry Hedgeko, whose old man worked in the Ford plant in Cleveland, Ohio. His father had a finger cut off on the assembly line and told anyone who'd listen that he was a Ford man through and through. My dad loved Cadillacs and used to say that FORD stood for "Fix, Or Repair Daily", but I never said anything about that to Jerry.

American car makers were changing car types so fast— creating changes in colours and trim, adding ornamental extras, it seemed, by the hour. Our parents were caught up in it all, convinced that to play their part in the pursuit of the American Dream we simply needed a new set of wheels every two years.

A monstrously roomy Ford Fairlane, with eight big cylinders set dream-seeking-families back $2280. And the sporty two-door Ford Mustang went for a whopper of a price at only $1999. Mind you, gasoline idled around six cents a gallon.

That bus sojourn was the best trip of my life, because on the way Debbie Kerr and Joyce Sabossli sat in front of us the entire trip. I was in love with them both, alternating days of affection in a kid-like "She Loves Me, She Loves Me Not" fashion where I just alternated first names.

It was over 350km (200 miles) to Dearborn and I was doing it with both Debbie and Joyce. In the dark on the way home, with The Beatles' song *I Want To Hold Your Hand* for moral support, Jerry changed seats with Joyce and I held Debbie's hand for nearly 200km (125 miles) without ever letting go once. For the balance of the trip, we played musical chairs again and I had my other palm-pleasured by Joyce. A double-hitter, all on the very same day.

Because of the field trip, there was no homework and I could lay in bed, stare up to the ceiling and just relive the entire journey of the heart. I considered the options of changing religions. I read somewhere Mormons were allowed to have two wives.

The Blind, Leading the Blind
Aussie Trevor Lake, in Europe

I was a tour guide in Europe. I stood up at the front of the coach, full of all the good oil on the flora, fauna, history and general culture. One day I was asked to lead a tour through the southern part of Germany which included a visit to Oberammergau (site of the famous Passion Play every 10 years). I had never visited this region before, neither had my coach driver, but I had my trusty field notes so I felt confident that nothing could go wrong.

As we approached Oberammergau, I told my driver to look out for a village where the houses had frescoes on their facades, and that in the centre of the village he would spot a monastery-like building with a large car park in front of it.

I turned my back on the front of the bus and began my spiel about the history of the plague and the links to the Passion Play some centuries before. I delivered a rousing tale that had my passengers passionately enthralled. I was headed for big tips and graciously delivered gratuities.

As the bus stopped in the car park I led my troops through the large wooden gates of the monastery and into the vast courtyard within. I told them to wander around and be back in half an hour.

One of them asked me where the stage would normally be. I had no idea so pointed in what seemed to be the most obvious place.

"Oh, that's odd," he said, "When I have seen photos of the Passion Play, there is always a range of mountains in the distance".

I told him they had moved the stage only recently to allow for more people to get into the audience. But at the same time, I also remembered these photos and now I was equally curious about the stage.

I went to the nearby curio shop and asked them where the stage for the Passion Play was.

"Oberammergau," the man replied.

I knew that, but where in Oberammergau, I asked,

casting my arm around the courtyard.

"Oberammergau," he said again.

A cold, icy grip came upon my heart as I asked, "Where are we now?"

"Oberau," he replied. "Oberammergau is actually the next village along the road."

I quickly gathered my passengers, told the driver he had stopped in the wrong village—and that when we reached the next one, he was to drive through as fast as he could. Meanwhile, I would engage the coach in a trivia quiz to distract them.

Amazingly, no one ever noticed.

Mistaken Identity

We took our three small children on a trip to California

We had just hopped off our 14-hour flight to Los Angeles from Australia, somewhat disoriented, and I insisted the entire family escort me directly to the car rental counter. I did the necessary paperwork, initialled in a zillion places and took possession of a lush Lincoln Towne car big enough to make a happy homestead for visiting refugees.

The massive car came with plush leather seats, seat warmers and that many cup-holders we were still discovering new ones a week into the trip.

Our hotel was booked for a sweet suite in Santa Monica and I know LA like the back of my own buttocks. So when we pulled onto Sepulveda Blvd. heading in the wrong direction, my African-born wife Bridget suggested we make corrections to our course.

Being a 'specialist' in most things American, I shrugged

this notion off and continued going the wrong way. When realty finally sunk in, I made plans to do a U-turn and admit defeat, which just so happened to be at a break in the roadway which boasted a massive "No U-TURN sign". Despite my navigator's warnings, I made the illegal turn and shortly afterwards noted the red-flashing lights in my rear view mirror. My wife, being gracious and from a very good family, never says stuff like "I told you so!" She just submissively shook her head, pretending to look in her purse for bail and bond dollars.

A young, crisp-uniformed and crew-cut California State Trooper approached the car and asked for my driver's licence and registration. I'm an American, but because we live in Australia I was required to secure a local licence.

I produced my Australian licence and delivered my best "G'day matey!" accent.

The trooper leaned into the luxury car, saw the jet-lagged kids at the back and said, "Do you believe that Crocodile Hunter? Is that guy for real? I watch his show all the time, and that guy's crazy!"

I struck a chord with the trooper, laying down my best Aussie imitation accent—and my sons, knowing that telling lies is wrong, attempted to chip in from the plush back seat about the fact that I was actually a proud American. I kept flicking an arm into the back seat, saying my off-spring were jet-lagged and requesting silence while I chatted with the nice officer. I offered up icy stares to my backseat boys, silently lip-syncing loudly, "NO POCKET MONEY!"

My two boys made numerous attempts to help me remember my place of birth—and as the gods would have it, I think our trooper might have been a bit hard of hearing. My wife Bridget remained silent, shook her head from side to side and made no attempt to silence our offspring.

The trooper handed me back my paperwork and with great gusto said, "Drive safely, obey the signs"... and topped it off with, "And in America we say, 'Have a nice day!'" as he returned to his patrol car.

I replied with a whopping big "G'day mate!", pulled away from the curb and put the big car on cruise control.

Bridget said later, when describing the incident to friends that car-makers really ought to invent a little accessory to automobiles that smacked drivers in the back of the head when they did stupid stuff. It would save millions of wives from having to do it.

Petrol Pornography
Mark Sheehan, The Sea of Cortez, Mexico

The weather was warm, the beer cold, the exchange rate exceptional, and there were many Canadian and American females who would fly south to tan on the Mexican beachfronts.

With my friends Shane and Jack, we would cruise the used car lots of Los Angeles for an old Dodge Dart, the preferred car of choice for Mexican cab drivers. We knew we could always find spare parts south of the border with this brand. For a few hundred dollars and a bit of haggling we'd land something suitable for a road trip south.

Our next stop was a nearby junkyard where we'd purchase a half-dozen old licence plates at a dollar a pop. In Mexico we often had licence plates stolen by the locals, so we used the wrong ones whenever possible and saved the real McCoy for when we ultimately returned to the US border.

The next pre-trip stop was the used bookshop in Santa Monica, where we'd relieve them of about 200 copies of dog-eared and previously played-with *Penthouse* and *Playboy* magazines.

We could buy these slightly soiled back-issues of smut in bulk for about 25 cents each, and in Mexico the locals considered them "pure gold". Just a few copies of porn would often gain us an entire tank of gasoline. A couple dozen titles could earn us a full oil and filter change.

We'd carefully plan every visit to the petrol pump, splaying out the centrefolds along the back window, body parts in plain sight of the local gas attendant, who in the course of pumping our fuel would be keen to negotiate a deal. Petrol for porn, we called it.

Proper Paperwork!
Cathy Nightingale, Lake Nakuru, Kenya

In Kenya, we are frequently stopped on the road by traffic police, supposedly checking vehicles for faults or irregularities.

On one occasion I was stopped and the officer demanded to know why I was not displaying the 80kmh (50mph) sticker (mandatory for Public Service Vehicles). I told him I didn't have to display the sticker on my car.

He insisted I did have to display the sticker, as my car was a station wagon. I told him that, no, I didn't have to display the sticker as mine was a private car, not a taxi, and I was not restricted to 80kmh —I was allowed to do 100kmh (60mph).

"Madam, you can do any speed you like, but you MUST have an 80kmh sticker," he said.

Road Worthiness and Roadway Wankers
Mark Sheehan, University of Cailfornia

When I was at college, I was living in a trailer that was shaped like a giant silver-sided turtle, and I needed to find alternative accommodation.

Dan Wright's dad was a local developer, but living at home was cramping Dan's lust for life so we rented a two-bedroomed apartment on Gutierrez Street.

It was in a pretty dismal area of Santa Barbara but it boasted a pool (the water tuned green a week after we moved in and stayed that way), a laundry room (with machines that ate quarters and spat back dirty laundry) and an easy walk to classes.

Dan owned a vintage 1960 VW Beetle convertible and was willing to take it anywhere for a lark, especially to the hot springs of Lake Cachuma where the locals girls were reputed to bathe naked.

The VW Beetle is the finest car ever built, because when it broke you knew what to do to fix it. I look under the hood of our car now, and I'm lucky to locate the dip-stick without directions. New fangled cars hide even the hood latches so you can't open it anyway.

But with an air-cooled 'bug', you could rig almost anything on the VW to make it get up and go again.

Getting to the hot springs required fording a few riverbeds, and on one these crossings the reliable car gave up the ghost mid-stream.

Dan fixed the broken accelerator cable with a piece of kite string and we continued undaunted. He's a smart guy, but the string was too short to reach the front seat. As the Beetle's engine was located in the rear end of the car I sat in the back and, on his command, applied gas or eased up when Dan needed to shift gears. It worked wonderfully.

We lolled in the hot springs drinking shared concoctions of dubious contents with nude women until we looked like a pair of sun-dried tomatoes. Life hardly ever gets any better, and with our two new-found female friends in tow, we headed back to town—me in the back seat controlling the gas, while Dan shifted and steered from the front.

As fate would have it, the California Highway Safety inspectors set up occasional roadblocks and stopped cars randomly to check road-worthiness.

And against all odds, we picked the exact day and location they chose to test Dan's mettle. Our trusty but somewhat wounded steed was waved to the side of the road for an inspection. These boys were decked out in white coveralls designed to crawl under cars and appeared frighteningly thorough. They checked the amount of tread on our tires with calipers, scrutinised our tyre pressure, lights, directional signals and pulled a tyre to determine the longevity of our brake pads.

I sat in the back seat, silently concealing the kite-string and smiling at my date.

When they completed their inspection, the top brass presented Dan with a Xeroxed copy of a "well done" letter, signed by the Governor, and said we were free to pass. Dan said something to the effect of "We're going now" (hint-hint). I discreetly pulled the kite string and away we went.

Two miracles in the same day.

Delivery Boy

"A tourist is a fellow who drives thousands of miles so he can be photographed standing in front of his car"
—Emile Ganst

There's an old photo of me, with hair creeping towards my butt crack, leaning against the metallic hood-works of a brand new, puke-green Cadillac Coupe de Ville.

It was my boss's car, jammed to the rooftop reading light with his wife's Miami-bound winter wardrobe. The rest of the space was crammed with a portable TV that weighed a ton and a zillion boxes of shoes from Bloomingdales and Pappagallo's on the Miracle Mile. I liked to pretend I owned the Caddy, but in reality I was just a long-haul delivery boy.

For a kid with a newly issued licence, and a need for speed, taking Milton's 367 horse-powered Caddy south each year was a bit of a vacation. I also got some nice cash in hand, a return airline ticket and free gas.

On one of these car delivery trips I stopped for gas at a single-storey steel building in Georgia, and the old man behind the counter asked if I'd like to "take my change upstairs". I thought this was totally odd for a building with only one level in the middle of nowhere.

I learned later that "upstairs" was the brothel owner's way of suggesting one should take their change and spend it on the ladies of the night.

I'd visited a Georgia whore-house and "filling station" and didn't even know it.

Stung at 70!

I'm such a stickler for fuel savings that I had flipped my Trek van's vents in, and cut the air conditioning down as my Trek group took a sandwich siesta after a big lunch break and swim.

We were in the desert area of Cochise Stronghold, the place where the famed Indian chief hid out from US calvary for years. The road was gun-barrel long, as heat waves of mirage came off the black top for miles and it was in the peak heat of August.

If I kept the van flying at over 130 kilometres (80 miles) an hour, we'd be in the camp's pool by 4pm, otherwise the 90kmh (55mph) speed limit wouldn't let us arrive until night-time.

When I was convinced everyone had nodded off, I slowly pushed the pedal to the floorboards and flew. With the windows wide open, hot air poured through the van and my summer shorts, so a good flow of air was circulating around my tanned midriff.

Suddenly my windshield was splattered with a coating of yellow puss. I'd wiped out an entire swarm of bees in one hit.

But the massacre of bees was not complete, because a few of them tore into the driver's side vent and embedded death stingers into my tender private parts. I yelped, lost control of the van—and it took about a football field to slowly pull over, hop out and survey the groin area damage.

In the struggle to regain the controls, I'd swerved the van from side to side on the deserted roadway, planting the young girl from Auckland's head neatly between my legs.

As Trekkers were jolted awake, they looked forward to

the scene of my young and scantily clad navigator with her head planted in my jockey shorts... In all, I'd been stung six times, and each of the stingers nestled under my skin only to remind me days later with hard, black lumps.

My trekkers were convinced I'd been having an on-road servicing from my co-pilot. And I walked like a bow-legged cowboy for a full week afterwards.

The U-bolt Cat!

My wife Bridget adopted a stray kitten on Staten Island that she called Gurdy, and when we moved from coast to coast we brought the bloody cat with us.

When we left Los Angeles, we packed our car the night before a big trip across the Nevada desert, hoping to be on the road before 6am, but friends came around with farewell drinks and gifts and we overslept, putting us in the desert heat in an old Chevy Nova at over 100°F (38°C).

The cat panted, tongue stretched out to the length of a number two pencil. And Bridget shot into a 7-11 convenience store for ice cubes when the cat stopped breathing. Gurdy cat was out cold, and I ran into the store, opened the ice cream freezer and settled her there. The manager raised a significant complaint about putting animals in his freezer and I threatened back. Our cat came back to life, squatted among the popsicles and peed, and we bought bags of ice.

Eight miles up the road we checked into a motel, turned up the air conditioning to polar settings and slept in until well after dark.

BEFORE DEPARTING.

A Strange Coincidence

An elderly couple was driving cross-country and the woman was behind the wheel. She was pulled over by the highway patrol. The officer said, "Ma'am, did you know you were speeding?"

The woman turned to her husband and asked, "What did he say?"

The old man yelled out to her, "HE SAID YOU WERE SPEEDING."

The patrolman said, "May I see your licence?"

The woman turned to her husband and asked, "What did he say?"

The old man yelled, "HE WANTS TO SEE YOUR LICENCE." The woman gave him her licence.

The patrolman said, "I see you are from Arkansas. I spent some time there once, had the worst sex with a woman I have ever had."

The woman turned to her husband and asked, "What did he say?"

"HE THINKS HE KNOWS YOU," the old man yelled.

On the long and tedious road trips, to break up the monotony my friend Tony church suggests: "Stop and collect the road-kill."

An Eventful Journey

An Englishwoman and her young son were travelling in a taxi in New York. As they were driving through a rather seedy looking part of town, the boy became fascinated by the garishly made-up women in short skirts and high heels, who seemed to be accosting some of the men passing by.

"Mummy," the boy asked. "What are those ladies doing?"

The mother, clearly embarrassed by the question, replied, "I expect they're lost and are asking people for directions"

The taxi driver overhead this and interrupted, "Why not tell me boy the truth, those women are prostitutes."

The mother blushed more brightly at this remark but the boy wouldn't let it go:

"What are prostitutes, Mummy? Are they like other women? Do they have children too?"

"Of course," the mother replied. "That's where New York taxi drivers come from."

Another bastard!

Road Rage

A father, who worked away from home, made a special effort with his family at the weekends. Every Sunday morning he would take his daughter out for a drive

One particular Sunday however, he was so full of cold that he really didn't feel like driving at all. Luckily, his wife came to the rescue and decided that for this week she would take their daughter out.

They returned just before lunch and the little girl ran upstairs to see her father.

"Well," the father asked. "Did you enjoy your ride with Mummy?"

"Oh yes, Daddy," the girl replied. "And do you know what...we didn't see a single bastard!"

Does this sound a wee bit like you?

A Few of our Favourite Driving Habits

Happily cruising down the middle lane of a motorway with either indicator flashing, but going nowhere.

Picking your nose and believing no one can see you.

Not realising that there is any other setting for your lights than high beam.

Indicating to move into a lane that you're already halfway in.

Falling asleep at the wheel, just in time for the lights to turn green.

Sounding your horn one nanosecond after the lights change to green if the car in front hasn't sped off.

Sending sprays of wiper wash right over the top of your car and washing the one behind.

Overtaking then pulling in front and slowing down.
Sharing whatever is on your car stereo with anyone within a mile radius.

The New York Taxi Driver

Father O'Flannagan dies due to old age. Upon entering St. Peter's gate, there is another man in front, waiting to go into heaven. St. Peter asks the man, "What is your name what did you accomplish during your life?"

The man responds, "My name is Joe Cohen,and I was a New York City taxi driver for 14 years."

"Very well," says St. Peter, "Here is your silk robe and golden sceptre. Now you may walk in the streets of our Lord."

St. Peter looks at the Father and asks, "What is your name and what did you accomplish?"

He responds, "I'm Father O'Flannagan and have devoted the last 62 years to the Lord."

"Very well," says St. Peter. "Here is your cotton robe and wooden staff—you may enter."

"Wait a minute," says O'Flannagan. "You gave the taxi driver a silk robe and golden sceptre. Why did I only get a cotton robe and wooden staff?"

"Well," St. Peter said. "We work on a performance scale. You see, while you preached, everyone slept. When he drove taxis, everyone prayed!"

5. SAILING SIX SHEETS TO THE WIND

The lure to get on the water is like an addiction for me. I've been known to fall into the water and occasionally I even drink the stuff straight from the tap.

A Leap of Faith—Broken Bones On The Erie Barge Canal
David Sheehan

New York Governor Dewitt Clinton opened the Erie Barge Canal in 1825, and I don't think anybody did much to repair it in the years after the ribbon-cutting. There were 36 locks and over 640km (400 miles) of the canal in total, and my old man dragged us through all of it aboard his boat the *Starling*. Twice!

In 1964 my old man bought a very big boat and nobody, not even him, knew what to do with it. Stopping it was only one of our problems. It was a two-masted, gaff-rigged sailing Schooner and we didn't know how to do that (sail!) either.

At 14 years of age, I discovered Coffee-mate™ on the maiden voyage, a man-made milk substitute. It had no redeeming qualities at all, other than the fact that it made my mother's coffee palatable. Our mother had thousands of redeeming qualities but making potable coffee was not one of them.

I also had my first peek at combustible pollution as I learned that Lake Erie was officially deemed a "dead lake"— and that the Cuyahoga River, which cut through the armpit of industrial Cleveland, Ohio, was so potently polluted it would often catch fire. I never knew a river could burn.

Our captain and father, "Big Dave", awarded me the position of stern lineman because I was built big for my age, and he figured I had the best odds of stopping 25 tons of small ship. My older brother Bob, extremely agile and fast-on-his-feet, looked after the bow line. While on deck, Cathy Chris, Mark and our mother moved fenders around by the command of our "captain" to keep the *Starling* from smearing its newly painted sides on slimy concrete lock-walls and unforgiving docks.

My assignment was to leap to the shore, wrap a massive stern line around anything I thought might hold fast and try to stop our small ship from slamming into stuff. I was good at it, about 50 per cent of the time.

Breaking my leg however, wasn't really my fault. I had jumped from our boat to a rickety dock in Tonawanda, New York and went straight through the rotten planks and into the oily drink. I was still holding the stern line tight, hoping to slow the progress of our small ship as it coasted on a collision course with the gas dock. Our father the entire time reminding me that from my current position, I was in no position to stop the *Starling*. He wanted me to stop fooling around and get to the task at hand.

In the Emergency Room, when our captain realised I'd be sporting a leg-long cast, he had the doctors embed a huge green rubber block onto the bottom, effectively converting my leg with me attached to it, into a human bumper. I was to sit topsides on the deck, and use my casted foot to "fend off", like a battering ram, any attacking concrete or dockage.

By the time we tethered the *Starling* to our home port dock in Manhasset Bay, New York, that big green rubber bumper had been worn as smooth as a baby's buttock stubble, taking some of the cast with it as it went. My leg is fine now and I hardly ever feel it, unless it's going to rain.

Skinny Dippin'!

My good friend Geoff Brain was the navigator on a ten-day, extremely reckless road rally across the Australian Outback. Called "The Great Escape", it raised over $500,000 for patient services and research for the Cystic Fibrosis Foundation, and I'd managed to convince Sir Richard Branson and his Virgin Airlines to sponsor our vehicle. Partly due to my disregard for safety and kangaroo wellbeing, he was reluctant to embark on a second rally.

One night under the stars, settled in our swags and after a few gallons of local grog, Geoff told me this story. Some body parts have been left out to protect the guilty...

Geoffrey and a few of his also-single mates had chipped in to buy a speed boat, which was a tops idea for attracting the attention of girls. And they'd become very proficient at offering up invites at the local pub to spend a pleasant day on the water with any women who presented as fair game.

On one occasion, they invited two lovely Swiss au pairs along for the day, and things were going along swimmingly. Eager to strut his stuff on skis, Geoffrey took his turn behind the tow line, smiled at the somewhat shy lasses and gave the helmsman a thumbs up to hit the throttle. And away he went.

The boat's motor hiccupped as Geoffrey sank to his waist on the skis—and when the boat took flight he resurfaced stark naked, with his trunks settled firmly around his ankles. Although the girls were unimpressed, the opportunistic driver decided to tow Geoff in front of a wedding on the yacht club lawn at full throttle and then around the shoreline for assembled families to enjoy.

After a good nine minutes of southern exposure, the local police boat appeared, blue lights flashing and the driver was fined for making an illegal wake in a NO-WAKE Zone.

The somewhat shaken Swiss girls asked the attending officer from the police boat if they could have a lift back to shore, and he accepted.

The girls were, according to Geoffrey, in a mild state of culture shock.

I never knew if he said this by way of bragging...

Pre-breakfast Boating

There is a message in this little boating trip; don't leave the pub well-lubricated at 3am and go fishing!

My buddies and I bought a boat in 1971 to fish on Long Island Sound. And after a night at the pub, we decided to take a joy ride.

I sat atop the front seat, with the salt air in my face, wind blowing my hair and pulling tears into the outside corners of my eyes as we sped at full tilt past the harbour lighthouse.

Beth, my good buddy, sat low in the seat, out of wind's way, and Chris, my co-boat owner, drove the boat at breakneck speed. None of us would have been clear to operate farm machinery at the time.

Like the snap of fingers, the steering cable broke, the boat went into a frantic left-hand turn and Beth's head ploughed into my leg and drove it through the side windshield. The boat spun uncontrolled for what seemed like hours, and when we finally got control I had shards of glass imbedded in my leg.

Blood was spurting everywhere.

I sat on the outboard engine for the ride home, steering the boat by moving my ass left or right. We spent a few hours in the hospital's emergency room where I added nine stitches to my bodyworks.

Because we had to return to the dock at trawling speed, we set out two fishing lines, and landed four Striped Bass and three Blue Fish in the process.

My gushing blood managed to mix itself in with the filleting of the fish.

The Human GPS

Norb Vonnegut, author and good buddy has written some fantastic books. And he tossed this one onto the pile for our enjoyment...

You know how we all have one special talent: the gift big enough to fill a room, or so subtle only we know for sure? I believe everybody has a knack, flair, call it what you want. We each enjoy our own superpower.

My wife is a human GPS. You could drop Mary in the deepest, darkest Amazon rain forest and she'd find her way home no problem. No area, domestic or international, is beyond her navigational skills and this includes the Italian city of Venice.

Equally enchanting as it is confusing, Venice city is to the world's tourists what the Himalayas are to mountain climbers.

Don't get me wrong. I love the place. There just happen to be enormous challenges touring the canals. And some are more serious than the navigation.

Several years ago, we were driving through Austria en

route to Italy. And true to form, Mary was scrutinising maps and reading a travel guide that described "marauding bands of Venetian pirates."

"Watch out," the guide warned. "There are thieves everywhere."

Duly alerted, we resolved to keep our eyes peeled but the "marauding bands of Venetian pirates" became something of a running joke during our drive. For that matter, the warnings seemed overblown upon arrival. There was a state-of-the-art parking garage on the mainland outside the water taxi stand. It was well staffed and well organised, the picture of efficiency. I think 747s would be lucky to receive the kind of guidance our parking attendants offered that day. No sign of bandits.

Right.

The drop zone for water cabs was our first hint something was amiss. Literally, it was a drop zone. The attendants—smiling and waving their arms in the manner that makes the Italian language so enchanting—guided us to the departure area, tossed our bags into the hands of the crew, and signalled for us to get in. Next stop, Venice.

There was one problem. The drop was eight feet. There were no stairs or ladders, just lots of air separating us from the deck. It was, as you might guess, the kind of moment that gave us dry mouth.

We did it, grasping the walls, allowing our bodies to stretch as far down as possible, and finally dropping. Me first. I helped Mary, who stuck the landing—a couple of feet, no big deal. When we were both safe, we glanced at each other with knowing looks that said, "This isn't right."

Then we waited. Our boat captain explained that another family was arriving, which made me wonder what kind of monitoring system the garage used. After about 15 minutes, the couple and their kids arrived. They, too, stuck the landings, both Mary and me helping this time. The captain indicated we would go to their hotel first.

We drove across the harbour, breathtaking views of Venice, and exchanged pleasantries with the family. Like us, they were staying three days. Inside the city's canal system, a turn here and a turn there, the captain announced to our fellow passengers with the Cheshire cat smile, "We're at your hotel."

That's when Mary kicked into action. She marched up to the front of the boat and stated, emphatic, resolved, 100 per cent certain, "No, we're not."

Our captain pretended not to speak English but he got the point. Mary gestured right, then left, and stabbed at her map of the canals with an insistent forefinger. He was cowered and—nodding his head with an expression that says "Yikes" in any language —started the boat again.

Mary tapped him on the shoulders when it was time to turn, her map and index finger at the ready. After twenty minutes, we arrived at the first hotel. The couple thanked us, packed up their kids, and left. They told Mary, "Thank you. We would've been lost."

Then came our turn. The captain turned down one canal and proceeded to a dock, which looked like all the others. "We're here." Mary folded her arms and shook her head, tapping her foot on the deck.

The captain shrugged and started motoring again. He had this guilty look on his face, like he should have known better than to try a second time. Twenty minutes later we pulled up to our hotel.

Phew.

In retrospect, I think we charged right into the marauding band of pirates from the guidebook. They wanted a quick drop, a quick buck and a quick getaway. I don't claim to have any special insights into pirates. But as pirates go, I suspect these guys were fairly agreeable. They just happened to meet their match that day:

My wife, the human GPS.

Cruisin' on Christmas Day
Paula April, Caribbean

My father's 80th birthday was coming and he and my mother wanted to take the family on a cruise to celebrate. As there are several teachers in the family and a crew of 16, Christmas Day was the most convenient and least expensive option we had...and so the reservations were made.

Along for the ride was the 82-year-old brother of my father, who was married at age 64 to his "hot" tennis partner Sandy. Now 85, Sandy still wore short tennis skirts as her daily Miami outfit, and my uncle was still smitten. What we were just learning is Sandy was in the beginning stages of Alzheimer's disease.

The photo was important to my parents, but it was quite clear that we were a motley crew. They were proud to be able to provide this experience for their children and grandchildren and wanted the proverbial family photo to cement the good memories (and to brag to their friends, no doubt).

We ran into trouble when we could not find even one area that did not have Christmas decorations in evidence.

We are Jewish to varying degrees. Raised culturally Jewish, my sister married an Israeli native, became observant and raised her daughters who married Orthodox men. On the other hand, I abandoned the religion and married two Christian husbands. My daughters were brought up celebrating everything.

So...Christmas decorations in this family photo was a no-no.

With a whiney baby in tow, we traipsed around looking for an appropriate venue. We found a staircase where we were able to move some of the decorations so as not to be in the actual photo.

We were in business!

The day of our family photo, 85-year-old Sandy was squeezed into a spaghetti strapped, bright red gown, equipped with ample cleavage that clearly made my orthodox nephews-in-law turn as red as her dress. My appropriately modest 20-something nieces, stifled by the warm Caribbean weather, wore long skirts, flat shoes, white socks, long-sleeved, high collar shirts and hats.

It wasn't until we picked up the photos two days later that we noticed that as the photographer snapped, Sandy, always ready for a pose, put her arm up high in the air and gave the photographer her best flirtatious smile and sexy pose! What a contrast to have two young conservative 20-somethings standing next to an 85-year-old sexy babe!

A normal red-blooded family we're not. Tolerant and loving in spite of our differences, we are!

The infamous 80th birthday cruise went so well that cruising became a family tradition. Now in their late 80s and always looking for the best deals, they found one that would take us to several stops in Central America and the Caribbean.

Sponsored by their senior living community, we met at the clubhouse and boarded buses for the port in Fort Lauderdale, Florida. We were delayed however, as one woman forgot her passport and had to go back to her apartment to retrieve it.

That was only the start of a slow-going, delay-filled week.

We had to turn the ship around three times to leave passengers ashore for medical reasons.

We were scolded for saying "excuse me" to a man in a wheelchair by his wife as they took up the whole hallway to get to the dining room.

My husband and I took a shore excursion. The bus was empty. The line to get on the bus extended out so far it was interfering in traffic. At the door, struggling to get on the bus was a hefty woman. The task of entering the bus was taking so much of her energy, that on the second step, she stopped, dug through her purse, unwrapped a sandwich and began eating it. Fortified, she then continued up the bus. No one said a word!

Then it happened to us! Leaving the ship one morning, the crew had dutifully washed down the gangplank, making them slick. My dad was in front of me and my mum was in front of him. He slipped on the wet surface, and on the way down knocked my mother off of her feet. They looked like two bowling pins going down to make a spare. Now you see them, now you don't!

No broken bones, but we did spend the day at a medical clinic in the British Virgin Islands. No loss as my parents received a free cruise as compensation.

The ship got into port 14 hours late! It was the slowest, yet most exhausting cruise we had taken.

6. SADDLE SORE

According to Wikipedia there are currently 58 million horses on the planet..
And they all hate me.

If you are ever offered a ride on a Harley, just plan to leave your panties on the side walk....

Mount Up!

I was leading a tour of about 25 South African schoolgirls through Jackson Hole, Wyoming at the exact same time about 7000 Harley-Davidsons arrived. The girls were naive and eager to climb onto the saddle of a thoroughbred or onto a Triumph Daytona to see what it was all about.

They attracted bikers like spaghetti to meatballs, and I sat up with baseball bats and the burly headmaster for two nights watching, to assure the girls stayed in the tents and were not tempted to go for a ride on the back of a Harley-hog. I'd already given a lecture on the Hells Angels over dinner. And breakfast.

We took the girls horse-riding during the day, and made them do a fair bit of hiking to keep them off the wooden boardwalks of town.

One afternoon I passed the Million Dollar Cowboy Bar, which features barstools created from western cowboy saddles. The saloon also features a million dollars in silver, laminated into the bar-top, nightly western bands and reputation for rough-housing.

And there, perched atop the saddle-strolls, were four of my finest gals, being entertained by a bunch of black leather-clad bikers. Grossly outnumbered, I entered the saloon and advised the bikers that each of the girls was underage and they could be jailed for providing drinks and offers of consensual sex to minors.

To put some powder in my punch, I added the fact that their South African fathers all toted firearms and had a way of seeking retribution for any offences caused to their loved ones.

The reply was swift, and I anchored myself for a pounding when the leader of the group said he was pulling down seven figures as a certified public accountant in Chicago. And further, that the girls were only drinking ginger beers and iced coffees.

My South African lasses had been adopted by the bikers, all of whom were accountants and lawyers from Chicago. They'd been plying the girls with soft drinks and sharing pictures of their own families and they had no intention of kicking my ass or chasing those attached to the girls.

As the bar was a popular tourist attraction, it allowed minors in for photo-taking opportunities during daylight hours, and the girls had stumbled in to take a picture or two when they struck a conversation with the "bikers".

In the end, there were about 20 of the bikers, returning from an annual road trip, and they came to the campground en masse—with all their colours and leathers on—and took the girls, the headmaster and I around the camp in turn, taking pictures for the kids to take back to South Africa. It just goes to show, you can never judge a biker by his leathers!

"One day your life will flash before your eyes. Make sure it's worth watching."

7. MATTERS OF THE HEAD AND HEART

Struck by the Taj Mahal
Trevor Lake, India

While the coffins of Shah Jahan and his wife Mumtaz are on display on the ground floor of the Taj Mahal, their actual burial sites are down in the basement. An area that is usually off-limits to tourists.

On my first visit, a scruffy looking tout asked if I would like to see the real marble tombs in the basement. I eagerly accepted and he led me down a narrow trapdoor and a steep flight of stairs.

"Mind your head," he said as he led the way with his flashlight.

Once at the bottom, he shined the light through the side of the tombs to show their translucency and gave me some garbled story that was barely comprehensible. I decided this tour was over and started back up the stairs. He grabbed my shirt and demanded money. I gave him a few rupees, but he thought it wasn't enough.

We argued for a short time and I decided this was getting nowhere, so I would simply do the manly thing and run away. I raced up the stairs and suddenly he turned off his flashlight, plunging me into total darkness.

It was at this moment that I remembered his earlier warning...mind your head.

I remembered it, because my head crashed into the ceiling made of solid marble. The thud was audible, and as my guide turned his light back on I saw his toothy grin. At the time, I was determined not to show how much it hurt, but three days later the doctor told me I had concussion from ploughing into the Taj Mahal.

I never bothered lodging an insurance claim. I didn't think the insurance company would believe me.

Paris on a Broken Heart
Lynsey McCaffrey, Paris

After a bad break-up, I decided to start my emotional rehabilitation process in Paris. This coincided with my recent discovery of *Sex and the City*, meditation and Shirley Valentine.

I was an independent woman on a mission.

I also considered myself fluent in French (I could tell people my name and that I liked black dogs) so I knew I would be fine. An impromptu trip, it lacked anything close to planning. I chose the first set of cheap tickets I could find, an even cheaper hotel and planned to spend the day walking the streets of Paris in a Carrie Bradshaw-worthy outfit and a copy of *Buddhism for Beginners* tucked under my arm.

I arrived at Charles de Gaulle airport at midnight. Dizzy from excitement at managing to leave England by myself (I was so grown up), I climbed into a taxi and decided this was the time to practise my French.

I have no idea what I said, but it culminated with the driver trying to convince me to leave my bags at the hotel so he could drive me around Paris and show me the sights. It was 1am and I had only just met this man. He didn't speak English nor my version of French...something didn't feel right.

I tried to recollect statistical data regarding which EU country had the highest percentage of serial killers. They didn't come to mind, so I declined his offer just in case.

I woke the next day prepared for the beautiful view from my hotel window. Instead I convinced myself that the trash bags and fornicating "chats" in the alleyway down below were so very Parisian.

Being an impromptu trip there had been one major oversight on my part: I had not considered the date I had chosen to travel.

Bearing in mind I was getting over a break-up, waking up alone in Paris may have been bad enough, but waking up alone in Paris on Valentine's Day was a huge faux-pas. Yes, Paris would be on steroids but it could only make me stronger...plus I was too stubborn to admit to my stupidity.

I was ready for my six hour walk. I would see the sites. I would breathe in the aroma of Paris and my pack of Marlboro lights.

After one hour I met my downfall. H&M and McDonald's. Not only did this absorb three hours of my day. It meant all subsequent photos of myself outside beautiful landmarks (proof of my "cultured" trip) were complete with my plastic shopping bags in hand and an expression of indigestion on my face.

I realised my lack of planning meant I had no idea where I was going. I may have passed the Louvre, but I couldn't be certain as I had barely seen any sites. To redeem myself, I did what any desperate woman would do. I bought a baguette, cheese, meat...and went back to the hotel room to meditate. I was cultured again.

Years later I thank the heavens for the advancement in technology. I regularly set up my laptop, draw the curtains...and with the sweet drones of Rosetta stone beginner's French in the background, I turn on Google Maps street view and finally walk the streets of Paris.

8. FOOD FIGHTS

The Maple Syrup Rule
Blaise Winter, Del Rio, Texas

Traveller's practical rule number 143A: "Never, ever put maple syrup in a bag in the overhead airline bin."

The slight lowering of cabin pressure at cruise altitude pressurises the syrup container, squeezing out the syrup into whatever is in the bag. It can be seen dripping onto a seated and very tall man's bald head, in mid-flight. Two hours later he'll reach up, taste the drippings and say, "Ooh, maple SY-RUP!"

This actually happened to me on a flight from New York to LAX.

Thanksgiving Fowl Play
Cathy Sheehan-Leslie, Sydney

Cathy is my younger and much-smarter sister. She could have written this book, and probably a few others, better than me. I give Cathy full credit for writing some of my very best A-papers in college.

The 1970s were post skyjacking, pre-9/11—and airport security often seemed to focus on contraband and illegal importation.

November 1979. It was my first trip Stateside from Australia back home to the east coast of the US.

In those days flying time for the trip averaged 39 hours—and I was determined to see my entire family because it might be ages before I was game to make that journey again! Somewhat of a Herculean task as my family is large and global, but despite being spread out geographically, we are remarkably close.

I was working my way around the globe, and had visited with relatives in California, Ohio, Boston and Philadelphia. Then I made my way to my mum, who had retired to central Florida. The plan was to spend some time with her, and then I was off to see my sister and her brood in Bridgetown, Barbados.

"Do you think you could take something to your sister for me?" Mum asks.

"Sure, Mum," I naively replied. "What it is?"

"Well, you know how important it is to her to celebrate Thanksgiving no matter where she is?"

I nodded yeah, and that is how I ended up being responsible for a frozen 10kg (22lb) smoked turkey with chestnut stuffing as hand luggage.

The trip between central Florida and Barbados was a logistical challenge. Ground transport to Tampa. Flight #1 from Tampa to Miami, flight #2 from Miami to Puerto Rico and, finally, flight #3 from Puerto Rico to Bridgetown, Barbados.

The logistical challenge morphed into a scientific conundrum when Mum added the element of keeping a frozen 10kg smoked turkey with chestnut stuffing actually frozen for the duration of the trip.

I was more than happy to let her figure it out. After all, I was just the turkey mule.

"Mum, this carry-on bag is really heavy."

"Well, I wanted to make sure that the turkey was big enough. I'm not sure how many people will be sharing the holiday with your sister."

Check-in at Tampa airport just after the X-ray of my hand luggage.

"Miss, can you tell me what is in this bag?" they ask, as

I am being moved away from the public area.

"Yes," I replied.

"Miss, did you pack this bag yourself?"

"No," I honestly replied. "My mum did," as I am being moved through swinging doors marked AIRPORT PERSONNEL ONLY

"Miss, what are the contents of this bag?" was their next question, asked in a small back office.

"It's a frozen smoked turkey with chestnut stuffing ...for my sister...for Thanksgiving."

It would appear that a frozen, smoked 10kg turkey with chestnut stuffing, solidly frozen and repeatedly wrapped and covered in aluminium foil, throws up an unusual image when sent through 1970s luggage X-ray equipment. An image that is pretty much non-identifiable—it could be 10kg of explosives or 10kg of illegal drugs or 10kg of frozen smoked turkey with chestnut stuffing—doesn't tell you much.

The final investigation of my carry-on bag and the turkey was completed just in time for me to make my flight to Miami.

Carefully re-wrapped, I was cleared for Miami.

Check-in at Miami airport, just after the X-ray of my hand luggage. Yep, you guessed it.

"Miss, can you tell me what is in this bag?" a very large guard asked as I am being moved away from the public area.

"Yes," I replied.

"Miss, did you pack this bag yourself?"

"No," I honestly replied. "My mum did," as I am being moved through heavy doors marked AIRPORT SECURITY.

"Miss, what are the contents of this bag?" I'm asked in a private interview room.

"It's a frozen 10kg smoked turkey with chestnut stuffing...for my sister...for Thanksgiving."

I made the flight to Puerto Rico but I bet you can see the pattern here.

Check-in at San Juan airport started with, "Miss, can you tell me what is in this bag?"...and finished with me just making my flight to Bridgetown, Barbados.

A frozen 10kg smoked turkey with chestnut stuffing still intact and frozen. And now I am taking the travelling feast international—with the Customs and Immigrations Department waiting for me in International Arrivals in Bridgetown, Barbados.

"Miss, what is in this bag?" asked a man with a Barbadian accent as I am being escorted from the public area by three very large uniformed guards.

By this time, I had a very real fear that the frozen 10kg smoked turkey with chestnut stuffing was going to be confiscated...and we had gone through too much together for me to willingly surrender it to any authorities and disappoint my sister.

I recounted my tale, in graphic detail, explaining that every airport checkpoint had authorised me to carry the turkey.

Eventually, despite literally seeing some of the staff of the Barbados Customs and Immigration and Security Service licking their lips in anticipation of perhaps scoring some portion of a frozen 10kg smoked turkey with chestnut stuffing, there was no additional "fowl play".

We celebrated Thanksgiving with traditional holiday fare! It was delicious...and it seemed none the worse for the radiation treatments en route!

Slap the Hand that Feeds You

My friend Robert Wagner introduced me to the best Indian food I've ever eaten anywhere. The venue was a bucket-shop of a storefront across the street from the Nation newspaper on River Road in Nairobi and you could belly up for a whopping 78 cents for the all-you-could-bivouac luncheon buffet.

Sometimes Bob would really piss me off, because he'd just sit back and let me learn shit on my own.

Even if it hurt occasionally.

In this Indian eatery you sat at long bench tables and were provided with a large silver tray as a plate. No one was given any cutlery, because you ate with your hands.

Waiters swooped like flies, rapidly dropping incredible ladles of curries, piles of podiums and pans of unknown origin into the tray. It was a bit like a Henry Ford production line of food.

The eatery was always packed with Pakistanis, Indians and other resident locals, and I knew I was doing something wrong when the waiters aggressively slapped my hand three times within minutes.

I was just about to spring up and start slapping back when Bob told me that in Africa, the left hand is reserved for toilet duties—and that's why I was being warned and wrist warmed.

I looked at my fellow eaters, and many were sitting on their left apertures. When I pointed out the fact that I was left-handed in the crapper, Bob said something about being in Rome among the Romans. When I eat Indian food now, I fall back into the habit of sitting on my shitting hand again.

Eating Out
Lisa Alpine, Northern California

Lisa is the author of Exotic Life: Laughing Rivers,
Dancing Drums and Tangled Hearts *and co-author of*
Wild Writing Women: Stories of World Travel

I was travelling over the Altiplano plateau on a gravel road that snakes around Lake Titicaca in Bolivia. The Indians there are extremely poor and the environment absurdly harsh (4000 metre or 13,000 feet elevation and freezing). There were no tourist facilities so I spent the night in the mud brick hut of an Aymara Indian family, who had openly invited me in to dinner.

They were eating what they ate every day of the year–chuños, tiny freeze-dried potatoes in weird mottled colours of purple, green and red. The potato originated in South America and there are more varieties in Bolivia and Peru than any other part of the world.

The dehydrated ones we were eating had been reconstituted with murky boiling water. No salt. No flavour. My hosts savoured them. These puny potatoes were a main part of their existence. When they weren't eating them, they were cultivating them.

"How are they harvested?" I asked, attempting to spark conversation among this very reticent and superstitious family.

The mother, whose mahogany face was cracked and polished from exposure to extreme weather, told me, "We dig them up when they are ready and leave them on the hard ground to freeze. Then we go through the field in our bare feet and roll each one under our feet to remove the skin. We store them in baskets and they last a year."

"Oh, really?" was my only comment.

I looked down at her feet. They were blackened and cracked and had calluses as thick as history books. Maybe I did detect some flavour in my meal after all.

Put Someone in Charge
Carlsbad Caverns, New Mexico

Every evening in summer, more than one million Mexican free-tail bats tornado their way out of Carlsbad Caverns National Park in the US state of New Mexico. Park rangers do an enlightening nightly talk and the event is remarkable to behold. The whirling dervish of bat-wings takes place like clockwork, just around dusk, and the bats emerge from the ceiling deep in the caverns some miles away.

I wanted my Australian friends to witness it, but not being able to attend two activities simultaneously I left Paul in charge of putting on the kettles for the spaghetti bolognese.

If Paul had to pick between the bats and his beers, he'd choose the brews every time. I had my heart to heart with him, and he assured me he had everything fully under control. Later, I realised that what he meant to say was that his cooler-full of beer was at just the right temperature for drinking.

When our group returned to camp after dark, Paul was sunk in my beach chair, surrounded by empties, friendly raccoons and skunks. The tipped cooking pot of sauce was already being absorbed into the New Mexico landscape. The pot filled with the pasta was still cooking at high heat, and the water had boiled off, leaving us with the largest single block of spaghetti that any of us had ever witnessed.

We tipped it out of the pot, and when it cooled to the consistency of an ice block, my Italian kid hit it with a hammer we used to drive tent stakes. And the hammer handle broke.

Paul was a great roof-rack loader, but I never sent him up there if he was drinking.

We ate breakfast cereal that evening, and everyone admitted the sunset bat trip was worth every kilo of pasta we had to pay.

For breakfast we ate bologna sandwiches and potato chips.

9. HOTELS, MOTELS AND CAMPING

"If a man does not keep pace with his companions, perhaps it is because he hears a different drummer. Let him step to the music which he hears, however measured or far away."
—Henry David Thoreau, in his book Walden

Heated Hotels!
Dick Turner, Belgium

Occasionally our tour company management had to do an airport pick-up of passengers that our London office seemed to forget about.

These pick-ups were simple, and I got to spend a few hours away from the lunacy of "operations". On this occasion I drove to JFK Airport in New York and met the passengers. My mission was to simply deliver them from the airport to the Prince George Hotel in Manhattan. It was mid-summer and the temperature idled near 100°F (38°C), even at midnight. Naturally the group's flight was late, but by 1.30am we had everyone accounted for.

It was a wee bit funny to watch these jet-lagged kids, weighed down with heavy baggage, walking through the revolving terminal doors from an air conditioned environment into a furnace of sweaty hell and humidity. Most of the would-be Trekkers did about 20 steps and folded over into a jabbering heap. The staggering and sweating trek to the vans took another 45 minutes to cover about as many metres. A metre every minute.

Eventually we had everyone aboard and all the gear safely stowed on the roof rack.

It then took us nearly one hour to get out of the JFK car park. For some bizarre reason every exit appeared closed. We drove round and round and round but our passengers didn't ever seem to catch on.

One and a half hours later, at 3.10am, the desk clerk at the Prince George proclaimed there had been a somewhat small reservation misunderstanding.

About half of the 24 passengers didn't have a room set aside. So, armed with information from an idiot at the

Prince George, we marched the stragglers off to The Martha Washington Hotel, about four blocks away. "They have rooms," he said. "Try there."

As I walked boldly into the Martha Washington lobby, followed by my baker's dozen of bed-less followers, we were confronted by an extremely hostile black security guard. He grabbed me by the scruff and hurled me bodily out onto the pavement.

It was then that I discovered, via a violent finger-waving lecture, that the Martha Washington was an ALL female hotel. Male species were not permitted to enter, under any circumstances.

Back at the Prince George Hotel, the smart arse who had suggested the Martha Washington grinned widely and said, "Oh yeah, right, I forgot."

By now it was after 4.30am and tempers were beginning to flare. Rooms were eventually found, and I made it back to The Manor just in time to whip up a few eggs and bacon.

At 8am the manager of the Prince George called and demanded that some of the Dutch guests we had delivered earlier be moved to another hotel right away. Post-haste. If not sooner.

Apparently, the air conditioning was not working in a room, so this Dutch chap decided he could get some ventilation if he opened the window. Remember, outside it was 100°F and humid. So he would not improve anything by opening the window...but without sleep who's thinking clearly anyhow?

Now this was an old hotel, what you might call student accommodation. The windows were old-style sash windows. Nevertheless the youngster managed to force open the window–and in the process, the 40 pound air conditioning unit plunged 30 floors to the pavement and splattered. By pure luck, and the fact it was early morning, it didn't kill anyone. However, the doorman was shaken and did take the rest of the day off.

The manager lost the plot, and we lost the contract with the hotel for the following season.

Clothes Make the Man
Trevor Lake, India

On the occasion of my wedding in 1996, the Indian Government gifted me with a fabulous five-star honeymoon, including the best suites in the best hotels and all meals laid on to my liking.

Unfortunately, halfway through the trip I picked up a rather bad case of Delhi Belly and fainted while sitting on the "throne", cracking my scalp open on the granite vanity.

The resulting wound required eight stitches. The doctor sprayed the open wound with some kind of "plastic" sealant, wrapped a vast bandage around my skull and told me not to wash my hair for ten days.

The humidity of the Indian summer saw us arrive at our hotel looking somewhat over-cooked, sweaty and very, VERY dishevelled.

On this particular day we were booked into what is probably the finest hotel in India, the Rambagh Palace in Jaipur.

After a week on the road, my bandage turban was bloody, stained and sat at an odd angle on my head. The porter took us to reception to check in. I noticed, on the far side of the lobby, a smartly dressed man who was obviously the hotel's general manager. He was surrounded by his senior management, a couple of girls with garlands and bowls of rose water and three well-decked-out traditional musicians.

His sour look across at me left no doubt that he was not happy to see this Chaplinesque tramp invading his luxurious lobby.

He sent his sales director over to reception.

"I wonder if you wouldn't mind the porter taking you to your room straight away, sir. You see, our general manager is expecting a very important VIP.

He called a porter and took my key from me... The Maharajah Suite, the top room in the hotel. His jaw fell open and he scuttled across to the general manager, who immediately ordered flower petals to be liberally scattered at my feet and for the band to strike up a rousing tune.

"Mr Lake," said the general manager, "it is truly an honour to have you stay in our hotel."

Just Another Pat on the Back!
Patricia Sheehan, Orlando, Florida

Several years back, Disney came up with a great timeshare idea that utilised points instead of blocked out weeks. I got in on the ground floor, and decided to take all my high school friends for a Disney girls' trip. I was unsure what to expect, but the price was right, so why not?

I put all the reservations under my name, Patricia Sheehan, and booked the Grand Floridian resort.

Upon arrival, we were greeted by the hotel manager, a butler and some dude driving us to our room in a golf cart, which was only about 15 metres away.

I was thinking, "Damn, all this for a lifetime cost of

$3000? Sweet!"

We were taken to the Sugarloaf building, which is the suite at Disneyworld where Princess Diana or Michael Jackson would have stayed.

Our butler has arranged lunch, drinks, more drinks and plenty of "on the house" Disney goodies. I think it goes without saying that within 15 minutes, we had demolished the suite in a way that would make rock star Eddie Van Halen proud.

Suddenly, after only three bottles of pre-chilled champagne there was a knock at the suite door. I was confident that it was our butler ,coming to confirm spa times.

But instead of smiley face butler, there stood Mr Grim Faced Hotel Manager, Mr Angry Security Man and a very beefy-looking, athletic woman.

The manager was a bit icy and demanded my ID. He scanned our group, noting the fact that we were all in hotel bathrobes and slippers, and that the food trays looked as if a herd of poorly trained Golden Retriever had been let loose.

Mr Angry Manager scrutinised my ID, sighed and "regretted to inform me of a terrible mistake."

It seemed the athletic woman in comfortable shoes behind him was Patty Sheehan, the world renowned professional golfer. She was engaged at a high cost to Donald Duck and Mickey Mouse to be a sportscaster for the Disney Golf Classic. And the room I and my girls were standing in, with all the goodies included was actually hers.

This was why I thought it to be strange when, on check-in, the concierge asked for my golf clubs at registration. Maybe that should have been my first clue.

At first I felt embarrassed, and then insulted that someone would confuse me for an older, lesbian professional golf player, and then like a greedy pig for already taking all the free room samples.

My friends and I had to change out of our robes and slippers, put back all the soaps and gels, and now it seemed like we were slumming it. No butler, no free Mickey Mouse stuff, and you KNOW there was no more champagne.

Disney sent us free chocolate strawberries a few nights later, but you could tell they were pity berries. We ate them anyway, complaining that our butler should have been there fixing drinks at the same time.

Horrors of Hotels
Andy Purvis, Scotland

Andy escorted me on a road trip north of Sydney to look at a bed-and-breakfast I had a fancy to buy.

The B&B was in the small Australian seaside town of Old Bar. The place I wanted to acquire boasted 18 bedrooms and nine baths, and two commercial kitchens. With a bad throwing arm, you could hit the ocean from any room. It was bit out of my price range to do by myself, so I hoped Andy would be willing to do the deal as a joint venture alongside me.

My wife and kids were already looking around for a leash with which to curtail my recent thoughts of an alternative lifestyle under the cover of "togetherness".

The week before our road trip, I tried to purchase a 40-hectare (100 acres) farm and my troops rebelled, saying they would never go there. Ever. They were beginning to look around for professional counselling. Someone I could talk to.

Because I spend so much of my time in hotels I've

always considered myself the definitive authority on what ails the hotel industry—and as the place was already a licenced B&B I thought of implementing a few changes. I thought I knew the pitfalls of the hospitality industry until I listened to Andy open up.

He started with hotels sporting uniformed bellcaps that offer great greetings, at the same time as they have a helping hand in your wallet.

Then Andy waxed lyrically about the plastic room keys afforded to modern-day travellers that never work on the first or second go. Especially for rooms that were miles away from reception. The closer you are to the front desk, the more reliable the plastic room keys become. Andy has a shoebox full of the old plastic keys he totes around, in the hope that one day he'll find one that actually works.

And in the classier hotels where Andy has laid his head, they give you a real key, often in real imitation gold with a corporate crest embedded into it, which guests like to take home as a keepsake.

So the classier the hotel, the bigger the ocean-going anchor they attach to the key as a deterrent to theft. A key which then bulges in one's pocket to make male lodgers look like guys who are toting big things around below their belt line.

Women, according to Andy, never carry these bulky passage keys because there is never enough room in their suitcase-sized handbags to fit them. It's always the guy who totes them. Andy has about a baker's dozen of these keys too, but he keeps them separate from the plastic ones in a glass cabinet.

On the return trip Andy offered to drive and continued to let fly on the pitfalls of lodging. I've gone stone-cold on the idea of owning the B&B. I let Andy drive, thinking this might take some of the pressure off the subject.

I forgot to mention earlier that Andy collects fast cars and faster motorcycles for fun. So instead of the therapeutic and calming effects of concentrating on the roadway, he accelerates both the volume of his discourse and the speed of our projectile.

Once inside your room, according to Andy, now driving calmly at more than 160kmh (100mph), the stay-over nightmares intensify.

The remote controls on hotel TVs nowadays require the level of understanding of Einstein or a rocket scientist, or the necessity to bring along on any romantic outing a teenager or two-year-old who know how the gizmos work.

The gizmos on the remote never do as they are commanded, and repeated calls to the front desk and reception only add fuel to the bonfire. When you do ultimately get someone from downstairs to come to your aid (hand out money please, Sir?), the game between Chelsea and some other city in England is already half over and you've missed the good bits.

I think Andy should be hired by hotels to tell them where they've lost the plot, and I tell him this in the hope that he will slow down to an idle at just under 160kmh. I tighten my seatbelt, re-check to be sure my airbag is enabled and decide it's time to try another conversational course.

Andy, I ask, what is it that you LIKE about staying in hotels. To which he replies faster than a speeding bullet with "very little".

Andy can go on a bit if you let him, and he went on to highlight the downside of bedside clock alarm radios that never ever work and front desk staff that forget to wake you at all, so you're in a constant state of anxiety about missing your flight.

Then we jump onto the jam-packed in-room minibar that requires a second mortgage to sample and, even worse, charges you for everything in there at the front desk when you remove items to make way for refrigerating the baby's bottles.

At 170kmh (105mph) Andy hits stride, as he glides my car through a series of speed cameras on the Mooney Mooney Bridge. (No I'm not making this up—go ahead and check.) He begins waxing lyrical about the lavatories in luxury hotels.

Andy is convinced that plumbing engineers all over the world come together at conventions to speak with one voice regarding the design of shower controls that either scald or chill users just for the fun of it.

He thinks these folks are frustrated at home so they conjure up the evil implements of just washing oneself off from time to time.

Andy suggests that is how an "English shower", which constitutes putting a warm and tested towel under one's armpits instead of brazenly stepping into the shower stall without body armour, came to be.

Needless to say, I didn't get around to buying that bed-and-breakfast.

Howard Johnson's Motor Lodges

Howard Johnson filled his chain of motor lodges by putting restaurants in front of them and taking pictures of the food you'd get when you ordered a burger. The pictures were the menu. You didn't even have to speak English to eat. You simply pointed to a picture and away went the waitress.

Howard gave America bug-free beds and a meal they could count on. Every motor lodge had a pool, rooms had TVs, and clean white towels and sheets. Rooms were rented by the night, never by the hour.

You knew exactly what you were getting for your money and your meals. Howard set a standard with his HoJo's and an entire nation embraced the notion.

Truck-stop owners seemed to be the only long-term losers in the offering, as many travellers used to look out for places where the truckers took meals, to avoid ptomaine poisoning or other roadside amebas.

I and my siblings felt spoilt when we got to stay at a Howard Johnson's motor lodge. We knew they'd have an ice maker in the lobby, a pool out the back (the pools were always freezing cold, a guaranteed Arctic temperature, but we'd swim anyhow) and a TV that had more than three channels on offer.

Parking the car precisely in front of our rented room was a must for our father, and after we'd drifted off to sleep he'd turn off the TV, open the plastic curtains, and sit vigil all night long.

In the early 1960s, we'd all heard horror stories of one-eyed road-side pirates who would steal your tyres while you slept. Sometimes, we were told, entire cars went missing.

Our father was not going to wind up being a *Reader's Digest* story, with cinder blocks underneath the family's Oldsmobile Vista Cruiser™ instead of his five-ply Firestones in the morning.

Nocturnal Hard Knocks
—Burned Bangers and Mash

The Mowbray Court Hotel was in the heart of Earls Court in London. Earls Court at the time was called the "Kangaroo Valley" because so many Australians bunked down there. A bed in the Mowbray cost about $15 a night and they tossed in an egg and cereal breakfast. Two tea bags for every 12 guests.

The place caught fire while I was sleeping in it. The fire got started by two long-haul Australian lads who'd had a wee bit too much grog to drink in the hotel's bar. They fell asleep with a small gas camp cooker going in their room after they had tossed sausages on it.

Everyone made it out of the place alive, and the two Australian lads graciously agreed to be exiled down the street to unburned quarters over the Lion's Head pub. My suitcase and clothing stunk of smoke for a good month afterwards.

Campground soakings
Del Rio, Texas

A film released in 1985 called *Lost In America* was a gone-wrong story of a couple who quit their jobs and decided to head out onto the open road in a Winnebago motor home.

The summer the film was released, TrekAmerica used a campground in Del Rio, Texas, so we could enjoy Lake Amistad cliff-jumping, a quick diversion into Mexico and a pool on the Mexican border.

The camping area was solid sandstone and sage brush, so we'd bring a bottle of Tequila for the old gal who assigned campsites and she'd pour herself a few shots before leading the way in her golf cart to our designated nightspots.

I'd discovered that the best way to secure the grass area surrounding the pool was to get the sunbaked gal drunk beforehand. I'd get my Trekkers to get into pool gear and let me apply a bit of lubrication to our hostess with my heavy pouring hand.

On one occasion, I'd over-lubricated our lass and she drove her cart straight up to the pool's edge and right into the drink.

She had miscalculated the time needed to take her foot off the gas and apply the appropriate brake. And with me following behind to the pool's patio edge, she launched herself and the cart over the grassy knoll of the pool area and straight into the deep end, but not before knocking one of my passengers off the diving board.

I had to jump into the deep end and pry her hands off the steering wheel, because she was still intent on driving. We put a tow rope over the steering wheel, and with the help of a half-dozen Trekkers pulled the golf cart out of the pool and onto the concrete.

The owner of the place, Bob, fired her every other week, but he couldn't seem to get anyone else to do her job—so they tolerated each other and the clever Trek leaders always got the good grass.

The old girl would even deliver a small colour TV to the site if there was good baseball game going on, and she'd have a free pour or more at every Trek table.

Bob had a gorgeous daughter of about 17 years of age, who was more than friendly with a good number of the Trek Leaders. She spent many a desert evening on the roof rack while Bob took the Trek passengers for a special tour of the real underbelly of Mexico, which included the "donkey shows", strip clubs and other sordid sides south of the border.

10. FAMILY FORTUNES AND IN-FIELD FIASCOS

"Take the Greyhound Bus and leave the driving to us!"

In 1961 President John F. Kennedy asked America to consider building backyard bomb shelters as the cold war heated up between the US and Russia. A year later, he was asking America to put a man on the moon. And bring him home.

The most popular TV shows that year were *Mr Ed* —a talking horse and *Rocky & Bullwinkle*, the moose-speaking cartoon characters.

Cigarette packs only had "freshness dates" stamped on them. And if you sent a "Dear John" letter to someone you wanted to dump, the postage stamp only set you back four cents.

That February was one of the coldest on record in Cleveland, Ohio, and my mother bought us all bus tickets to our grandparents' place in Lake Wales, Florida. Disneyworld was only a twinkle in Walt's eye back then, but we had glossy brochures for Cypress Gardens and I'd never seen a real palm tree before.

I didn't care. I liked the notion that they called Florida the "Sunshine State" and I was going. To this day I detest cold weather.

We took the express bus, which only stopped to refuel and change grey-uniformed drivers in key slums of America. I discovered stewed prunes and Jell-O™ could be purchased from automats in the sad bus terminals that ate my quarters.

The entire trip took 26 hours and I was introduced to "white only" water fountains and discovered that sand nettles hurt like hell on bare kid-feet. I also learned that rich people take the train. And they never live near inner-city bus stations.

The thing I remember most about that trip was the fact that the brochures lied.

The "Sunshine State" of Florida pelted us with rain for five of the seven days we were down there!

But I recall it as some of the best fun I'd ever had with my siblings alongside me. And at least it wasn't cold. Our father flew in, loaded us all into Grandpa's 1956 Ford Fairlane and drove us all halfway across the state to visit Bush Gardens.

On the way there, we all played games and told jokes, and I didn't care if we'd simply driven around in circles. I loved travelling "Digga-Digga" with my family. Our father told a whopper of a joke about a nun falling down stairs and everyone with the exception of our grandmother roared with laughter.

Nine hours later, on the return journey our grandmother burst into fits of laughter, and our father pulled to the side of the road thinking she'd wet herself. She'd been contemplating the joke for hours and finally, figured out the punch line.

Better late than never.

She was a wonderful grandmother, even if she cheated at cards. And chess. She left me out of her will.

Holidays with Kids! Or Not?
Tracey Spicer, Sydney

Tracey is a beautiful and talented Australian newscaster, writer and investigative reporter. She also is a great mother.

The American humourist Robert Benchley once said there

are two classes of travel: first class and with children. The former is characterised by fine wine, foie gras and a bit of slap and tickle; the latter by whining, a lot of slapping and the occasional tickle. But sometimes it's the parents who deserve a beating.

Take our family trip to Morocco, circa 2009. While most sensible folk would take their kids to the Gold Coast, Fiji or Disneyland, the Spicers decided to travel for five weeks through the north of Africa.

Fortunately, we managed to combine both classes of travel by engaging a VIP tour company—By Prior Arrangement—to sort out the particulars. They included camping in the desert, a beach house on the Atlantic Coast and a Kasbah in the Atlas Mountains. Perfect.

Except for the last day when we decided to "free range". In the middle of the medina in Marrakesh there is a place which can only be described as a kaleidoscope of humanity.

The Djemaa el Fna throbs to the slave songs of the Senegalese; young acrobats desperate for dirhams, soothsayers and bards and cobras performing their dance of death.

It was intoxicating—until I remembered we had two small children in our care. "Under no circumstances are our children allowed to go near those rabid monkeys on chains or those poisonous snakes," I hissed at hubby.

But the medina is a mysterious and magical place.

I turned around to find my four-year-old son kissing a monkey on the lips. The three-year-old was resplendent, draped in several snakes. Fortunately, they had been de-venomed (or so I was told). What is it about travelling that makes you lose all sensibility?

At home it's "don't forget to wear your seatbelt" and "hold my hand to cross the road". In Morocco, the

Philippines, Mauritius, the Cook Islands and several of the United States, the rant became "Relax! What's the worst thing that can happen?"

Well, racial vilification for one thing.

In Manila, Taj fell in love with our tour guide. Stroking her arm one day, something suddenly clicked. He stood up on a chair in the restaurant, pointed at her and said at the top of his voice, "You're BLACK!!!!!!!!!"

In Vanuatu, Grace spent the entire time pointing at large local lads and saying, "Daddy, Dada!" These are the stories with which we will blackmail our kids in the future. "If you don't clean up your room, I'll tell all your friends about the time you (insert embarrassing story here)." As a parent, that kind of behaviour is in a class of its own.

Parental Discretion— Pass the Peas, Please!

Stuart's wife Dana told me she was raising three kids if she took into account her husband. Her family of four was all part of a first-ever, modern-day wagon train of Recreational Vehicles (RV) I was trail-bossing around the National Parks of America.

It was the best tour-guiding assignment ever, with our free-wheeling recreational vehicles scurrying around independently during the day and rocking up for meals in very cushy campgrounds and RV resorts by night.

All I had to do was point good people in the right direction each day, and be sure I had the billy boiled and the beers cold when they arrived at dusk.

It was all very family friendly, and our merry band of

young angels always had a surprise or two brewing for me as the trail boss. The kids taught me things that never appear in guide books or child-rearing reports. So I learned about water-balloon shoot-outs at ten paces and "Let's see if we can drown the trail boss in the campground's pool", followed closely by "Let's put some poison oak on the trail boss's chair to see if his ass can swell up any bigger than it already is" games.

Stuart, Dana's 32-year-old "kid" was also pretty high maintenance. He had to have a nightly fire, and was stomping-his-foot-disappointed when I broke the news that he was legally barred from starting a bonfire in the Circus-Circus RV Resort on Las Vegas Blvd.

Stuart reluctantly caved in when I promised him a huge flame in the wilds of Bryce Canyon National Park, where they had entire forests for frying. Until then, we let him work through his frustration by playing with a box of wooden Red Head™ matches.

One dusk, after our crew of recreational vehicle families had circled the wagons, completed their sightseeing rounds for the day, plugged in the air conditioning and logged on to the international internet, everyone opted for a dip in the lush pool.

The kids suggested playing a new set of games with me, including "Take the trail bosses' glasses so he walks into walls", "Pour pool chlorine into his cold beer" and "Let's drown the trail boss!" adventures.

Stuart's two boys Ewan and Kade towelled off early and shot their entire wad of pocket money in the campground's general store, buying up wooden rifles that fired reinforced rubber bands at the speed of light.

They also commandeered the help of the other kids in the camp. Before I knew what had hit me, I was running for cover with whopping big welts and locking myself in my Cadillac camper equipped with all the creature comforts.

I looked like I had the mumps. A quick review of my situation bought me to the notion that I had enough food and beer on board to hold up indoors for three days if necessary. My fresh water tank was showing a satisfying 150 litres (40 gallons).

Shortly after the little terrorist renegades dispatched me they turned their attentions elsewhere and attacked Stuart. Not being one to take things lightly when it comes to retaliation, he belly-crawled in the dark to my camper, and together we slithered to the shop just before closing and bought a pair of the most deadly pea shooters ever manufactured in China.

I could have taken down a galloping gazelle with the little pea zapper.

We also armed ourselves with about 3kg (7lb) of uncooked peas each in plastic bags, as part of our arsenal. We took the tin lids off the campground's trash bins to serve as shields and attacked under cover of darkness. Smoking citronella candles covered our approach.

Those little terrorists hardly knew what hit them when we rushed the campfire and disrupted the cooking-of-marshmallows-beyond-recognition-ceremony that evening. Like the rubber bands, the peas left little red welts that lingered around for days.

The big difference was that our attack was based on sheer volume. The kids used two rubber bands at a time and then had to retrieve and reload. Stuart and I could easily fire-off a few hundred rounds a minute with our peashooters. We nailed it and, OK, we did create a bit of havoc in the campground after "quiet hours". Hey, we were on vacation so what the hell.

Stuart's wife took our peashooters away from us a few days later, saying that someone could easily get an eye poked out. This statement of confiscation was delivered while Dana was skilfully putting a butterfly bandage over her son's left eye, which required four stitches the next day in town. They had good travel insurance so we figured it was no big deal.

On the last day of the tour, Dana reluctantly let me have my peashooter back. I had to pinkie-promise to never, ever, ever shoot at anyone above the waist again. Ever. Naturally I crossed my fingers behind my back and swore.

Stuart's peashooter got nabbed going through customs when the family returned to Australia.

We're having a barbecue and reunion of the group soon, and I'm bringing the peas!

Water Shortage!

Bob Sheehan works for a government agency where he got his wish to carry a loaded gun when he likes. We make him lock it in the glove box of his car when he comes to dinner, which is, sadly, only about once every seven years. Like the Locust.

It was actually a warm sunny day in early June of 1955. School had been out for a week and the whole northern hemisphere summer stood before us.

It had been a summer tradition while we lived in Manhattan to spend the summers in a beach cottage owned by my mum's parents in Rocky Point on the north shore of Long Island. The fact we lived in Fabius, New York, did not deter our trek one bit.

For those of you not familiar (or don't care) about New York geography, Fabius is located just south of Syracuse in the central portion of the state. This area, to city residents, is known as "upstate"—by which the city-slickers and urban inhabitants refer to any area of New York state north of the Bronx.

In those days, the New York State Thruway was not complete, so the only way to travel the 500-plus kilometres (310 miles) was by back country roads.

In 1955 this meant a gruelling full day's drive starting and arriving in the dark. Accordingly, in the early dawn hours Dad loaded the Ford ranch-wagon with everything the family would need to see us through the summer.

This was not a small task.

Besides the normal clothing needed by this mass of people, we had to accommodate blankets, towels, assorted beach toys, bedding and baby Cathy's full-sized crib. It could only be accomplished by folding the back seat down and loading the car with all the "soft stuff" on top, so that we kids and our dog could lay on top of it and ride as best and as comfortably as we could. (Bear in mind that there were no seatbelt laws in those days.)

Dad, Mum and Cathy rode in the front while Ann, Dave, Mark, Ginger and I entwined arms, legs, bodies and paws as best as we could to fit atop the load. We eagerly started out heading in a generally southeast direction toward the Grand City Of New York with anticipation of sunny days, warm beaches and salt air.

The early part of the day started pleasantly enough, but a couple of hours into the trek someone started to complain that someone else was hogging more than their fair share of the available room. Clandestine pokes and jabs became prevalent as only five kids under the age of twelve could invent. When Ginger passed gas, Mum deemed that a pit stop was mandatory. We pulled to the side of the road and disembarked.

Mum had prepared snacks and drinks for lunch because feeding seven people on the road was just as expensive (allowing for inflation) in the mid-1950s as it is now. After alfresco dining and walking the dog, we reloaded and continued the journey. The afternoon and distance passed with a lot of discord, but no actual bloodshed recorded.

At dinnertime we were in the northern reaches of New Jersey heading for the George Washington Bridge, when Mum decided we should find a place for supper. In rural areas (pre-McDonald's) roadside eateries were few and far between, with little or no choice in the type of food offered. One ate what was available. We came upon a Chicken-in-the-Basket emporium between two towns whose names I forgot, if I ever knew them.

As we disembarked, the patrons and staff were treated to a scenario akin to a group of clowns getting out of that tiny car at the circus. We all (except Ginger) entered the restaurant and helped the staff rearrange the furniture to accommodate us all. This also necessitated returning to the car for Cathy's high chair as she would not agree to any other seating arrangement and made her objections widely known. (Cathy was never shy).

The meal commenced with everyone trying to order something different than anyone else due to sibling rivalry, but Dad made a deal with the cook to bring food out family style. In short, we ate.

After dinner, when Dad had settled the bill, we went out to continue the last hours of our journey. First we had to reload the high chair, which somehow could not fit back in the prior location so the car had to be re-stacked. As we got back into the car, Mum gave me a bowl and told me to go back inside and get some water for Ginger. When I asked, the cook stared at me and announced to the remaining occupants of the establishment, "My God, they have a dog in there too!" Patrons stood up and peered curiously through the windows.

I went out with the bowl of water for Ginger, which she lapped greedily. When the bowl was empty, I went back inside for more water. The cook observed that Ginger must be mighty thirsty. I then informed him that Ginger had had enough, but her eight puppies born in late April were now in need of water as well. At this point the crowd went wild and some came out to verify the improbable tale. Two bowls of water later, parents, children, dog and puppies piled back into the Ford. As Dad turned the ignition, Mum sent me back into the eatery. I walked up to the cook and asked "Please, may I have another bowl of water?

"What is it for this time, the cat?"

"No", I said, "Mark stepped in the goldfish bowl."

After the gales of incredulous laughter died down, all diners and staff ran outside to see for themselves. As we departed the lot we were treated to a loud and joyous ovation with many wishes for a safe trip.

All together the trip took almost eleven hours. Now, almost 60 years later, I still remember that one trip and that Chicken place better than all of the many road trips before or since.

The Happiest Place on Earth...
For the Happiest Day of My Life

Brian O'Heir is the only person I know who has memorised the Jack Kerouac book, 'On the Road', word for word.

"Yes!" she said after I popped the question. The next question, "Where?", was far more daunting.

Compared to almost all of my friends I was a little late in the marriage stakes—and nudging 40, this was my first wedding as opposed to my second or third.

So, what would we do and what sort of aisle would we walk down? A veteran of the traditional wedding, my partner was vocal on what she didn't want. Weddings, as far as my jaundiced view was concerned, were gatherings of long lost and often best forgotten relatives, not to mention friends who believed in wedding invitation reciprocity as a condition of friendship.

Most importantly of all, there was my partner's eight-year-old daughter to consider. Having been an integral part of my life for the previous five years, she had to be the icing on the wedding cake.

I worked in travel so somewhere special should be easy (and discounted!). Marrakesh maybe, Paris possibly, beach hut in Bali? The answer came from my American best friend and future best man.

"My wife is director of Disney Fairytale Weddings in Los Angeles," he casually proposed.

Magic!

I mentally ticked the boxes—no hint of tradition, total control of invited guests, enticing to an eight-year-old girl—and asked, "How booked up is April?"

So, it was decided. We would be the second Australian couple to have a Disney Fairytale Wedding. In the Rose Garden of the now demolished Disneyland Hotel we exchanged our vows beneath a sunny California sky before a celebrant, a handful of guests and a gushing, somewhat theatrical Minnie Mouse.

Little girls love fairytales and ours was no exception. Add the enchantment of Disneyland itself and you have a recipe for fantasy overload. Imagine a day of being the flower girl at your mum's Disney Fairytale Wedding, the chance to hang with Minnie Mouse—and, to top it off, being escorted through and around the National Barbie Doll Convention, which is coincidentally taking place in the auditorium next to the wedding luncheon venue, with Minnie Mouse.

Only in America!

Back home after a three week driving honeymoon criss-crossing the magnificent American southwest, I returned to my job as the marketing and product manager for an Australian travel wholesaler with responsibility for contracting North America product.

One of my first scheduled meetings was with a sales delegation from Disneyland California. After taking us through the range of new products, their piece de resistance was their new brochure for an as-yet untried product in Australia—Disney Fairytale Weddings. "It works in Japan, not sure about here," they reported.

As the Disney Sales Manager reached for her Fairytale folder that detailed the promise of wedding that only dreams are made of, I gasped, "Hold that thought, I want to show you a photo from my office."

And like any good fairytale, we are still living happily ever after.

Guns, passports and money!
Dr Laurence Frank, Berkeley, Masai-Mara, Kenya

Frank was a wonderful, left-of-field researcher when Earthwatch supported his spotted hyena research project in Kenya and sent this tale.

Our little campsite compound was composed of a canvas cook tent, a dining hall and eight other look-alike green tents, each equipped with tubular aluminium field beds.

Within fair scenting distance, we had also created a canvas porta-potty ablution block which included a long-drop toilet area. For added security, we strung nylon line around the perimeter and tied empty tin cans to it, to discourage nocturnal visits by the abundant elephants. The place was right out of a movie set for *Out of Africa*, nicely nestled across the river from the famous Maasai Mara game reserve.

After months of bribery and red tape, getting government permissions and securing camping rights, gun permits, prescriptions for horse tranquillisers (even though we had no horses), two chase vehicles, dart guns, the hiring-and-sobering-up of a well-loved Kamba cook and three Kikuyu nightwatchmen who came complete with poison tipped arrows and other necessities of life, we were ready to welcome our first troop of American volunteers to help with our Earthwatch spotted hyena project.

The group of well-scrubbed volunteers invaded our little canvas kingdom on the banks of the Moro River with all the trappings of upper-class America. Everyone boasted Ultrabrite™ smiles and straight teeth. Our well-heeled and enthused helpers were all ready to get hyena poo under their fingernails.

Still, the group was a little bit on edge and they said so. They'd been reading recent and shocking newspaper reports of marauding bandits and mean machete gangs prowling the region. And they had American passports, expensive cameras and American Express travellers' checks to protect.

To set them at ease we introduced them to the watchman staff, the nearly-sober, knife-wielding cook and then led them to the gun safe. The gun safe was a real beauty and weighted-in at over 40kg (90lb) on its own. It had three huge locking posts for the cover.

To assure its safety, we secured it to the fender of a Land-Rover to protect our volunteers' valuables, our 800 rounds of ammo, cameras and cash. For extra measure we'd anchored the massive gun vault to a pearl necklace of eight fully-inflated spare tyres on steel rims, woven around a good ten metres of heavy towing chain. The entire lot was anchored at the other end with a massive lock and key to a camping trailer. This is where the very pregnant Mrs Frank slept.

The night watchmen were gathered around the fire pit, a few metres away. But the real insurance policy was the fact that we were fully under the protection of the landlords, a well-respected and powerful Masai tribe who controlled the entire area. They had zero tolerance for cattle-eating lions on their land...or for unwelcomed guests.

The Moran, chiselled good-looking young warriors of the tribe, had all killed a lion, and they would not tolerate invaders of any shape or species.

We all slept wonderfully for nights on end, until one morning when we woke up to find the entire gun vault, the metres of thick chain and the eight fully inflated tyres all missing. Laurence got on the radio immediately to alert the district commissioner to the fact that over 800 rounds of ammo, two rifles and a 12 gauge shotgun were now in the hands of banditos, and the reply was not positive.

The commissioner was furious and threatened deportation. He was not pleased to be assembling a posse to try and apprehend the gang and gear before harm could be inflicted on Kenyan citizens.

He would be petitioning for our permits to be revoked and our visas to be cancelled. Turning over such an arsenal to the bad guys was not an event that earned a slap on the wrist warning.

While waiting for the district commissioner's troops to descend and give us our eviction notice, we were shocked to see 11 ochre-covered Masai Moran lope into the centre of the camp compound at a jog, like a millipede in line, toting the full ten metres of chain necklace, the eight fully inflated tyres and the gun chest intact.

It appeared our hosts and young landlords, without any local lions to kill of late, had run short of daring challenges, so they had plotted to take our valuables as a rite of passage and a showing of bravery.

They stole our gear just long enough to impress the tribal elders and their girlfriends. They were aware of our firearms and our fully armed nightwatchmen, and had been keeping us under surveillance for some nights, waiting to apply their plan.

Not a single lock head was tampered with and our entire inventory of ammo, documents and enough cash to buy an entire herd of cattle was as safe as it was when we had left it.

When the district commissioner arrived an hour later, everything was as it had been before. The Masai Moran ran off, in single file with the lope of gazelles, and our thanks... and, the price of two goats and a cow. They also made a promise not to slip off with our goods again in future..

The anger of the district commissioner was also abated after he killed an entire bottle of Johnnie Walker Blue Label scotch and sent his troops home a few hours later, happily well fed and watered. They meandered up the dirt track.

When it appeared as if even the feeding and the scotch was not going to be sufficient to stay our expedition's execution, Sandy, the cute blonde from Santa Barbara, flirted with him, and we photo-documented the DC's change in mood with Sandy perched on his lap, blouse opened three buttons, in a canvas camp chair.

Just in case we needed to send a note or two to his three wives.

11. CULTURAL DIFFERENCES

The Classic Photo
Trevor Lake, Sydney

This short submission was lodged from a BlackBerry while Trevor Lake was on his tractor.

In western Thailand, on the banks of the Mekong River, there is a cliff-face covered in Neolithic paintings. While I was visiting this stunning attraction, a group of monks was also sightseeing.

What a classic photo opportunity, I thought. The saffron robes of the monks against the ochre paintings of the cliff.

However, being a polite tourist, I did not want to offend the monks, so surreptitiously I started taking photos of them when I thought they were not looking. No matter how hard I tried, none of the shots came out right. Either they had their backs turned or someone would walk in front of me as I took the shot.

When we got to the end of the path, I dejectedly gave up and started to walk back to my car. One of the monks came running after me and sheepishly asked, "Would you mind having your photo taken with us. We wanted to do it earlier but we didn't want to offend you!"

There's A Sucker Born Every Minute

One particularly cold winter I decided to escape England for the comparative heat of Israel, where I spent three months travelling around.

I was in a youth hostel in the Galilee area and saw a note on the notice board saying they would offer free bed and board to anyone volunteering to help out in the local drive to reforest the area.

I explained to the boss that I had no experience in forestry but would like to help out. No problems at all, he assured me, and asked if I could use a camera. After telling him I was quite a good photographer I got the job.

I was led into an open garden, in the middle of which stood one rather puny looking sapling in a pot, and in front of that sat a cardholder. It turned out that this lonesome plant was the sole survivor of the reforestation programme.

The boss then handed me a long list of names and explained the job. I was to fill in the preprinted card with "This tree was donated to reforest the Galilee by..." I was to fill in the name of the wealthy benefactor, who was normally a New York-based Jew.

My instructions were to take the photograph, and at the end of the week the snapshot would be sent off to the New Yorker for him to proudly display in his wallet.

I was then to fill in another card, remove the first one and take another snap, for another unknowing New Yorker to show off to his family and friends.

During my stay, that puny little tree was sponsored by over a hundred well-meaning saps in the US. But it was only a brief stay. On the fifth day I awoke to find brown and dying leaves on the sapling—and not wanting to be accused of killing the goose that laid the golden egg, I left after breakfast!

Secret Weapons
Debbie Brooks in Europe

Debbie Brooks was the shapely bombshell who sold "Certified Yankee Hater!" T-shirts in front of Boston's Fenway Park, making a killing and dating a few of the Red Sox baseball players in the process. Debbie reminded me of this story, which happened in 1978.

I was 25 years old when I heard about Pan American's $50 Round Trip flight offer to Europe, so I decided to take my gal-pal Irene.

We flew to London at the tail end of the plane and enjoyed a few days of sightseeing before heading off to Paris. We walked the streets, soaked up all the atmosphere and headed to the Eiffel Tower to meet some French boys, just like we had been promised by the stories of our friends.

Instead of meeting the French males we were "guaranteed" to come across, we met two young Arabs. Or to be more specific, two Christian Lebanese men engaged in the battle of Beirut—which we only found out later. When we met them they were just a couple of hot young guys hanging at the Eiffel Tower —and within hours we were riding in their Mercedes.

Irene, riding shotgun, was looking for a map when she opened the glove box only to have a handgun fell out. She freaked!

I kinda liked the guy I was with so I insisted Irene "just chill". We ended up staying in their apartment for the night, looking at propaganda about the war in Lebanon. We were both actually relieved we made it out the next day and caught a train to Amsterdam.

When the train stopped in Belgium, the police came on board to check for terrorist connections.

We both freaked. We were convinced we had been flagged by these guys and that somehow we were carrying microfiche. Maybe our new male friends had targeted us as innocent Americans and planted "spy stuff" on us as carriers?

When we arrived at Schiphol airport in Amsterdam, there were several hundred young people who had also bought the $50 travel incentive. And all of them were threatening to riot and send the entire airport into complete chaos.

To distract us from what we were convinced was our impending arrest by Interpol, I decided to organise the group by getting folks lined up—identifying who had food, money and other travel necessities. All the while, I was scared to death that we were carrying some horrible terrorist microfilm.

It took three full days to get all the passengers on a plane—but when we did, they sang songs, had a communal pot luck and ate some of Pan Am's best food for free.

Once we arrived in New York, Irene and I were almost crying, thinking that we were going to get caught for espionage. So we ran to the ladies room and started tearing apart our bags.

Finally, we found it!! The spy package was a tube — fairly short, not like anything we Americans had seen. It was a newfangled European tampon!

To my relief, Pan Am gave me a free flight to Europe and a few hundred dollars as a way of thanking me for coordinating such a chaotic situation for the airline.

Local Knowledge

In my backpacking days I found myself in Chiang Mai, northern Thailand, where I was looking forward to my trip to one of the colourful, local hill tribes.

But it was obvious to me that this was a really touristy thing to do. I wanted the real thing, the off-the-beaten-path stuff, so I went to the local bus station the next day and waited until some colourful hill-tribe people boarded a bus and followed them.

An hour later they disembarked and, leaving the tarmac road, headed off into the jungle. I followed them at a safe distance, and from the rough state of the track I was convinced that this could only lead to a remote and non-touristy village.

Forty-five minutes later I was rewarded with the sight of a village in a clearing. My hopes that this was truly "off the beaten track" were reinforced when the local kids giggled as I tried to photograph them and hid their faces. This was a sure sign that they were afraid the white man's camera would steal their soul.

Indeed, I might actually be the first white person to ever enter the village! The kids led me to a large hut where, sitting on the floor, was a wizened old man smoking a large pipe. I sat before him in awe and delighted in our attempts to communicate.

A few minutes later I became aware of someone standing behind me. Turning around I saw a French woman wearing high heels, full make-up and what looked like a cocktail dress.

Stunned, I asked her how on Earth she had got here. She led me outside...where she pointed to the air-conditioned tourist bus and 20 of her compatriots. I was, it turned out, in the main village that tourists visited from Chiang Mai. And, unlike my misguided attempts the local kids were gladly posing for photos, ONCE they got paid!

I asked the tour guide if he would kindly give me a lift back to town. He refused, so I had to retrace my steps—now through the rain—to the main road. I waited many hours, soaked to the bone for a local bus.

Lebanon Stopover
James Olsen, San Miguel, Mexico

We were on our way to do interviews for a book that ended up being called *Exiles From the American Dream*. We had made the deal with the publisher, Sam Walker, with a handshake over lunch in our New York garden.

The last stop from New York to Kabul, the location of one of our interviewees, was a four-hour layover in Beirut. My co-writer Anne, courtesy of her grandmother, always hired a driver that would be ours for the duration and, even though it was supposed to be only three hours or so until the Air Afghani desk opened, she thought we should see Beirut.

Standing in the muggy air and feeling like I was in a sauna, I agreed...if the car was air conditioned.

Well, there was a clean looking car with signs of air conditioning. We asked the driver if he would stay with us for the trip into Beirut and the gold souks. I looked him over and he agreed to take us, so we piled our stuff into his trunk and took off for the city.

Nemo spoke no English and we knew not a word of Lebanese but the two guys decided they could manage in French. Nemo was a good conversationalist and as we drove down the highway we noticed kilometres of barbed wire fencing stretching into the interminable distance.

"Why the fence?" I asked Nemo.

"That's where the Palestinian refugees are kept," he said. "There are tens of thousands of them and some have been there for decades now. There are children born in there that have never been on the outside. At least they get food every day."

Anne directed Nemo to take her past the sites and to the gold souk. Beirut was a beautiful, active city and the souks were bustling. Nemo pointed out the famous Hotel St. Georges and the Phoenicia hotel, and told stories about who stayed in them. Due to his French he often got fares to those places.

He also regaled us with stories about the wonderful upcoming cultural events and the shopping in Hamra other than intricate gold bangles sold by the weight, not the workmanship. Anne explained there was no more time and we should head back to the airport. But she asked Nemo to wait half an hour to see if we were able to board our flight to Kabul.

Inside the airport was bedlam, except for the Air Afghani counter which was shuttered tight. After asking around we were told to come back tomorrow. They clearly weren't flying today and ours would have been the last flight out.

Worlds Apart

Nemo was waiting where we left him. I decided we should get a hotel room so we could shower, he could get a drink and we could sleep. We had been up about 30 hours at that point. Bedraggled, tired and hungry, I asked about a room only to be told there were no vacancies. Anne walked up to the concierge and started to cry.

"We will be here only one night," she pleaded. "Our flight to Kabul was cancelled. We will sleep in a broom closet if we have to."

"One moment, madam."

The concierge returned to explain he could let us have some Saudi prince's suite but we would have to vacate if the Prince appeared. We agreed. Escorted like the royalty we weren't, we followed him into a mammoth suite with a double king size bed, sheeted in silk. There were fresh flowers and fruit baskets all over the place.

"Enjoy yourself," the concierge winked.

Clean and refreshed we woke the next morning and started calling Air Afghani. When that didn't work we tried the unhelpful US Embassy. Finally Anne called our office in New York so that they wouldn't think we had vanished off the face of the Earth.

Anne's sister, Cathy, worked for us during college summer vacations and she answered the phone.

"Sis, thank God. We thought you were caught up in the coup."

"What coup?" Anne replied.

"It was in the *New York Times* this morning that there has been a coup d'etat in Kabul. They have overthrown the king."

Since we had a month to do our project we then decided to stay until the prince showed up or a plane took off for Kabul.

Trusty Nemo was waiting for us when we walked out the door. Over the next four days we had a silk robe made for Anne, sunned by the pool, listened to Claudio Arrau concertise in the ruins of Baalbek, and sat and dangled our feet in the Mediterranean in Byblos while the guys smoked grass.

We even went up the mountains to Harrisa to visit Our Lady of Lebanon, where Nemo bought Anne a small medal of the Virgin and put it on her watch. We spent a night at the casino watching gross, drunk Russians consume more vodka than we thought the country could import!

Eating Out

I kept myself busy with Nemo, making phone calls and trips to the airport to see if and when a flight was ever going to leave for Kabul. Meanwhile Anne dreamed of following all the road signs to places like Damascus, Sidon and Tyre.

Finally there was a rumour that one flight might be leaving the next day, so Nemo offered to take us home to dinner as it might be our last night.

We drove up into the mountains among the famous Cedars of Lebanon. An hour later we arrived at Nemo's home to be greeted by his mother and young wife. Nemo was Maronite Christian and his wife was Muslim. Mama was breaking her in to the traditions and foods of the family. We never figured out how they knew company was coming for dinner but endless dishes of delicious food kept appearing. Most of the meal was vegetables they grew at home. We sat at a large, old wooden table and a fire blazed to warm the room.

Towards the end of the meal, glasses of arak started flowing. Anne was used to it, as her family drank anisette or absinthe around the holidays—and while she loved it, she drank it slowly. I wasn't crazy about the licorice flavour but kept drinking.

With Nemo, I went out to the terrace overlooking the Mediterranean. "Look, Nemo. I want to pay you for the trip back to town and to the airport tomorrow and I also want to include a big tip," I said. "You have been so generous with your time and hospitality."

We settled the price of the fares and Nemo thought awhile about the tip.

"We like to hear the world news and music," he said, "so I would like a radio for the family."

The request was so sincere that I agreed on the spot.

Once business was taken care of, out came a pack of dark Turkish cigarettes. Anne was invited to join us for a smoke and the other women cleared up. She got lost in the smoke and the magical view.

What's for Desert?

Nemo asked me what I thought of Asma, his wife. I said I thought she was very beautiful and seemed very sweet and willing to please. He suggested we might like to spend the night at their house.

"Jim, you could spend the night with Asma and I could entertain Anne. She is also very pretty."

Anne came out of her reverie in time to see an amazed and shocked look cross my face. When she asked what was going on, I shook my head. Should I explain to Nemo about liberated American women not responding well to being treated like cattle?

"Nemo, very hospitable offer, but I am exhausted," I replied. "I drank too much arak and need to get up for the flight in the morning. We should head back now so we can pack."

Sorry, but no swingers' party for me, Nemo!

Nemo showed up the next morning and Anne thanked him for everything. He parked, unpacked the car and walked us to the gate. He actually waited until the plane taxied away from the gate to be sure we were safely on our way. No mention was made of the offer of the night before.

Every time we saw photos of Beirut being destroyed we ached a little, for the city, for Nemo and for Asma.

Numerous New Years!
Allison Anderson, India

I love to fly on New Year's evening. It often means flights are empty, cabin crews are generous with the pour and there is plenty of room to spread about. And I often get two shots at the same celebrations! You've got to love that International Date Line!

Allison Anderson travelled to India through the Rotary Foundation Cultural Ambassador Fellowship in 2001. She practises sustainable architecture in the US state of Mississippi and is always looking for opportunities to travel.

My travel companions and I had been on flights for days, travelling from Mississippi to Mumbai. As we left Heathrow, heading east, we realised not only that we would arrive near midnight on New Year's Eve, but that we could celebrate the New Year in each time zone along the way.

When we arrived, there was the typical chaos of a foreign airport: unknown customs, money exchange and baggage retrieval. The wait for our bags was quite extended, and people were restless to be away with their families. We could hear celebrations outside. The luggage hall was marble-tiled and quiet with exhaustion, but the muttering began as we waited.

A young man lifted the flap on the conveyor to see if anything was happening, and shouts rose from inside. I had time to see open bags and frantic searches by the baggage handlers before the flap was lowered, but the bags began to arrive immediately.

Two of our group had locked their suitcases, and those locks had been broken and the contents overturned. We would discover that all electronic items had been pilfered, but only from the locked cases. There were items sprawled everywhere, and to add to the situation one of my travel companions shouted to the other: "ARE THOSE YOUR UNDERPANTS ON THE CONVEYOR?"

We exited into a rush of taxi-wallahs, all clamouring for our business. We were to spend one night in an airport hotel, and the only man in the group, an older Sri Lankan returning to Asia for the first time in years, went back inside to find coins and call for the shuttle. That left four young women on the curb as the midnight hour struck, surrounded by men chattering in English, Hindi and all manner of dialects. Our general lack of enthusiasm hardly dampened theirs, until the pink shuttle bus arrived from the Orchid Hotel and they melted away.

The short ride from the airport to the hotel fulfilled all our stereotypical expectations of India. The slums of Dharavi are right there. Even in darkness we could see a tremendous gap in the city fabric: handmade enclosures, common water taps, children sleeping in the open, watchmen guarding refuse piles, the clutter and density of human inhabitation within circumstances hardly imaginable to us.

It was our New Year's Eve, but not their Diwali celebration, so there were some fireworks, clusters of people sitting around fires and children playing late in the darkness. All this activity was contained on one side of a smooth new highway lined with billboards for mobile phones and Bollywood movies.

The infrastructure was built to get tourists from the city to the airport on new tarmac, and a wall to hide the teeming informal settlements from the view of those tourists was sure to follow.

Beam Us Up, Scotty! Time Travellers

We pulled up at the Orchid, and it was as if we had magically teleported right back to London.

We entered the lobby's multi-storey atrium. A party was underway in the second-level disco, and there were beautiful Eurasian women in high heels and short skirts, accompanied by young men in bespoke suits, drinking champagne and laughing.

The elevator was filled with these ephemeral creatures, so we left the girl who had over-packed two huge duffels and humped our single cases up three flights of wool-carpeted stairs. At the rooms, we were confused by the eco-feature requiring the room card key to be inserted for lights and ventilation—it was 2001, but none of us had seen this system before.

The amenities were fabulous—spa settings on the tub and showerheads, fluffy towels and, of course, western toilets.

It would be a long time until we saw such luxury again as we traversed the country.

We became accustomed to the juxtaposition of abject

poverty and profligate luxury, between the extensive natural resources and intensive degradation of the land. We stayed in private homes, racetrack clubs, restored boat houses, political guesthouses, ashrams, and in Pondicherry we were guests in the Governor's mansion.

Every place told a story from a civilisation more ancient than our own and a place long inhabited.

Our preconceptions were gone by our second day in India, in this puzzling place where everyone had a mobile phone and no one a landline, where infrastructure was elaborate (except where it didn't exist) and where neighbours across state lines couldn't communicate unless they did so in English.

I discovered that adaptability is the most useful thing to pack.

Ear Apparent! A Matador, a Famous Author and an Ear
Anne Olsen, In The Mountains, Mexico

It was July 1960, the Feria de Julio Valencia festival, and I was a 16-year-old girl from the United States.

The festival was seven days long, with daily corridas part of the celebration. Seven days of bullfights and I had never been to even one. I was on a grand tour of Europe with my indomitable Spanish grandmother who was born in the province of Valencia. We were staying with her best friend and her grandchildren.

The corrida got off to a good start. We entered the plaza in horse-drawn carriages dressed in traditional Valenciana outfits. Once we were seated, the toreros entered, gorgeous in their traje de luzes. A bull exploded from the toril and it was all a glorious spectacle, with men seeming to dance as they swirled their bright red and yellow capes. Until the picadors that is. When they started jabbing the banderillas into the bull, the big animal got angry and charged the picador's horse, throwing it into the air.

Horse-crazy American girl that I was, I started to sniffle. Before I could break into a gasping sob, I felt a very hard pinch on my thigh.

Grandma hissed into my ear, "You cry, you disgrace the entire family and I will disown you."

I gulped back the tears and suffered through the rest of the corrida.

Grandma also arranged for one of the very good-looking grandsons to "explain" the bull fights to me. It worked. I was hooked on both the grandson and the corrida de toros.

I sat in the front row one sweltering afternoon and dropped my fan. A tall, bearded guy wearing a baseball hat with a camera hung around his neck handed it back to me.

"Mil gracias, señor," I said with the proper lisp.

"It's OK, kid," he replied and climbed into our box.

"Who is he," I whispered to my mentor.

"He the famous American, Ernesto Hemingway, writing something about Ordonez," he whispered back.

I was distracted by the entrance of a cute 18-year-old matador named Paco Camino, and I watched him gracefully take down a bull. In his second fight of the day Paco performed a perfect veronica. I fell in love.

That night, on the way to a ball, my date asked how the corrida was. I animatedly explained Paco and his veronica. As I was twirling my long skirts (I had no cape handy) I fell down a curved two-storey flight of stairs. The god of teenage girls was with me and I landed like a perfect flower with my chiffon skirts billowed around me.

My date flew down the stairs and gently picked me up to find the heel of my shoe broken off. He called the night porter and sent him, with the shoe, to wake up the local shoemaker and have him fix the heel so we could continue our evening and dance.

At the party, he told the story of the American girl acting out the veronica and falling down the stair. All evening, whenever anyone would trip or knock over a glass, everyone yelled, "Paco Camino!"

I was mortified.

In the wee hours of the morning, during a dance, my partner stepped aside to allow none other than Paco Camino to whisk me across the floor.

The next day, Paco fought two bulls again. His last was fantastic and the judges awarded him two ears and a tail. As he made his triumphant way around the ring, he threw me an ear!

Everyone seated near me cheered and the famous American writer leaned over and said, "That's real good, kid!" The next day a bull tossed my new hero.

I never saw Paco Camino again, but 30 years later a package arrived from my grandmother. Enshrined in a small jeweller's box was a desiccated bull's ear.

12. AWKWARD!

"Romeo, Romeo, where art thou, Romeo?"
"I'm down in the bushes. The damned ladder broke!"

Elevated Elevators
Randy and Donna Freed, Sausalito California

Mike Freed owns some of the very best beds on the planet with his Post Ranch Inn at Big Sur, about halfway between Los Angeles and San Francisco, and The Cavallo Point Lodge at the base of the Golden Gate Bridge. Mike sent me this newsletter from his brother Randy

Dear family,

It started yesterday as Donna and I were on the island of Madeira, Portugal. We left for our 10am flight from Madeira to Lisbon, so we could catch our connecting flight to Malaga, Spain. Our 10am flight was delayed for five hours because of "personality problems" with the crew.

Because of the delay we missed our 2pm flight from Lisbon to Malaga, and there were no other flights that day to Malaga. In fact, the next flight out of Lisbon to Malaga was the next day, leaving at 10am and arriving at 12.30pm. The problem with this is that we needed to be in Malaga no later than July 12th in the morning, as our Delta flight was scheduled to leave for JFK at 11.30am, Wednesday morning. Donna got on the phone to the insurance company. Nothing was accomplished.

After arriving in Lisbon and checking out all the other airlines we decided that the only way to get to Malaga and our onward flight was to rent a car. Unfortunately, no one at any of the car rental companies seem to know how far it was to Malaga, Spain from Lisbon. And, to top it off, since we needed to be able to drop the car off at the airport in Malaga, we had to find a car with a Spanish licence plate. The cost to rent a car was nearly 600 Euros (about $770).

When Donna and I were in Spain to start our trip, we rented a car for nine days for 400 Euros ($510). I was shocked but had no choice.

We get the car with three-quarters of a tank and with our GPS, we started our journey from the Lisbon airport at 10.15pm at night, on a drive which turned out to be over 725km (450 miles) in a geared car. Thank goodness we were able to listen to our GPS get us away from the airport, the city and onto the freeway, because less than two hours into our drive the GPS stopped working. The only other item we had was a Portuguese map. I don't read Portuguese, but we were told that there are many 24/7 gas stations along the way in case we needed gas or maps.

When we did find them, they failed to tell us that there are no toilet seats on the toilets. This didn't bother me but for some reason, Donna wasn't too pleased. Also, have you ever noticed that the biggest cockroaches come out at night and populate gas station bathrooms?

We finally made it to Malaga at 5.30am and then spent the next 30 minutes driving up and down the streets looking for our hotel that was opened 24 hours, except for answering their phones.

We finally arrived at 6am. We check into our room a little after 6am and schedule a wake-up call for 7.30am so we would have enough time to take a shower and have breakfast so we could leave for the airport by 8.30am. I decided not to go to sleep for fear of not being able to wake up and Donna slept for only 45 minutes.

At 8am, we get a call from our daughter Danielle in Santa Barbara, to let us know that she received a recorded message telling us that our 11.30am flight to JFK has been delayed until 3.30pm. I can't believe this. After driving the whole freakin' night to get to Malaga so we wouldn't miss our flight to JFK, it is now postponed an additional four hours.

With this four-hour delay to JFK, we will miss our connecting flight from JFK to SB. So instead of eating breakfast, Donna gets on the phone to Delta and tries to make other arrangements for our flights, but there is no one at Delta who speaks English, except to say, "Call 10am speak English." 10am. Finally Donna and United agree on a flight, but it will now cost us $150 per ticket to make the change.

At 10am, Donna calls Delta and speaks to a representative who says, "Why aren't you at the airport? Whether or not the flight has been delayed, you have to be there by 10.30am to check in or else you will lose your place."

Mad Dash. No breakfast. Donna and I stuff our two big suitcases, one small suitcase and our two carry-ons and rush out. While I have Donna check us out of the hotel, I go to pack the car. As I go out to our car, I stop. There is a bus behind our car loading a group of disabled people in wheelchairs, and there are stickers all over the front and back windshields of our car. I am not sure what the stickers say as they are in Spanish, but they weren't welcoming notes.

Speed forward. As we pull into the airport we get a recorded message from Delta that now says our Delta flight from Malaga to JFK was cancelled completely because of mechanical problems. They have scheduled us for a flight the next day. Now, unless we can make other arrangements, we will miss our United flight from JFK to Santa Barbara which we had just paid $300 to change.

I drop Donna off at the terminal so she can check in and get us another flight, as I am not staying, and I go to drop off the rental car. I take the luggage and go to the elevator where I meet a mother with her two daughters. Off we go, but not very far as all of a sudden there is a joint and the elevator stops.

What the F---?? I am now trapped in the elevator. It is nearly 11am. It's boiling hot in the elevator and we're trapped. Please pinch me so I can wake up. We sound the alarm. No one comes. We sound the alarm again and again and again and again. No one comes. We bang on the door. No one comes. I yell, "Help!! Anyone." They yell, "Ayuda!!" No one comes.

It's hot, musky, dirty and a little uncomfortable. Alright, a lot uncomfortable. I find the tone on my phone and call Donna. It goes into her voicemail. I call again and again and again. Each time my calls go to her voicemail and what goes through my mind? "Shit, each call is costing me 99 cents and she isn't picking up."

Finally, I make an executive decision.

If it's 11am in Spain, its 2am back home in Santa Barbara. I call Danielle. I wake her up and tell her I am trapped in the elevator at the airport. Try and reach Mom. Danielle says she call Donna seven times (that's $6.93) and each time she gets Donna's voicemail. So Danielle makes an executive decision and calls Abbey and Jamie, who are in touring Eastern Europe and are presently in Prague.

She says, "Dad is trapped in a elevator and I can't reach Mom, so can you try?"

(Ching, ching, ching...99 cents a call.)

Finally one of the daughters in the elevator, who speaks a little English, calls their emergency and explains what is going on. They call the airport, who call security, who call maintenance and they finally come down and pry open the door to the elevator. Except we are now somewhere in-between floors.

The family, who I have now become friends with (yes, you do bond with people in an elevator), wants me to leave and I say no. I help the mother and her two daughters out first, hand them their luggage and then, with the maintenance personnel I am helped off lucky-last. I go to find Donna somewhere in the airport.

In the meantime, Donna is starting to panic. She is consistently calling my phone (ching, ching, ching) and cannot reach me. She has me paged over the PA system at the airport and I don't respond. Donna is now thinking I must be injured or have had a heart attack—since I been up for over 28 hours, haven't eaten in 18 hours and cannot be reached. Finally we are reunited nearly one hour after I dropped her off at the airport.

In the meantime, because our flight has been cancelled, Delta is now putting all the passengers up in a hotel near Malaga and providing us with lunch, dinner and breakfast. While at the hotel, Donna spends the next three hours redoing our flight with United and seeing if either United or Delta will help accommodate us.

Delta will not accommodate us with our flight from JFK to SB because it's a United Airlines ticket. United will not accommodate us because these tickets were bought with frequent flyer miles and they blame Delta.

I want to go home. I start clicking my heels and saying, "There's no place like home, there's no place like home".

Donna gets on the internet, and 30 minutes later she finds a Delta flight from JFK leaving tomorrow (Wednesday) afternoon to Salt Lake and onto SB, where we will get in tomorrow night around 11pm for a total of $524 (she was able to trade some miles).Now tell me why the airlines couldn't have done this?

It is nearly 9.30pm (my time) and I have now been up 40 hours straight, too hyper to sleep. We are on the fifth floor and I refuse to take the elevator.

Anyway for me, I have learned a couple of worthwhile things from this experience:

1. If you use mileage or thank you points that you accumulate from your credit card, if there is more than one flight you have to use the same airline.

2. Only go to English speaking countries. This includes England, Scotland, Ireland, Canada, Australia, New Zealand, Fiji, the Scandinavian countries, Israel and Canada. I am sure there are a few more countries, but for me this is plenty.

And the reason for all this? Have you ever noticed that whenever a problem arises or there is an emergency where you are, no one nearby speaks English. Absolutely no one

Potty-Training
Les Cox in Eastern Europe

Les Cox is British and has been living in Australia for the past 25 years. He got his start on the road with Contiki Tours

While travelling around Eastern Europe in the mid-1970s my mate and I arrived at the Yugoslavian border, with both of us desperately needing to use the loo after a long day on the road.

We saw a sign that seemed to look like "Toilet" but the two entrances were in Yugoslavian. Which was male and which was female? That was the big question.

"Easy," we both said. We'd wait cross-legged for a local

to walk in one and that will show us.

With bladders bursting finally an old woman arrived and waddled into one entrance, and we smartly sprinted into the other.

We were greeted by a long raised row of two well-worn wooden planks to sit on. Charming we thought. Very old worldly. A pit below caught everything.

So holding our breath, we dropped our trousers to the ankle and sat down. Next minute my mate burst into laughter and points over my shoulder. At the other end of the row sat the old lady smiling away at us both. Yes–two entrances, one toilet!

"Thanks to the interstate highway system, it is now possible to travel from coast to coast without seeing anything."
—Charles Kuralt, US journalist

The Monster Dildo of Mexico
Lisa Alpine , Northern California

Paul leads adventure tours to Baja, Mexico annually. Last winter, the group was heading back to the States and stopped at a hot springs overnight somewhere near San Felipe.

Wencil, one of the trip leaders, is a handyman sort of guy. After fielding a bunch of complaints that the toilet in the men's camp bathroom didn't work, he went to investigate.

Something was blocking the flow of water. When Wencil lifted the tank lid, he adjusted his eyes in the dim light and couldn't quite fathom what the object was that was stuffed into the tank.

Pink, long, wide. It was a gargantuan dildo, just hanging out in the toilet bowl tank.

Wencil gingerly removed the obstruction. He didn't want the others in his group to see him sporting this rubber wonder, so he wrapped it in a towel and made sure its head wasn't sticking out. Not knowing what to do with it, he then hid it under his sleeping bag and zipped the tent shut.

Sitting around the campfire that night, Wencil had a hard time keeping this new-found thing a secret. He invited Paul to his tent when most of the others had gone to bed and presented this new addition to Paul.

After five minutes of disbelief and a running stream of "Oh my God, Oh my God, Oh my God," Paul, who is very social and loves to stir things up, took the torch, so to speak, and presented it to the people still gathered around the campfire.

After rolling around in the dirt in hysterics, the group voted to place the almighty lingam on the breakfast table and deck it out altar-style for the breakfast crew. Flowers, candles, and beads all adorned the now out-in-the-open phallic totem.

The next morning, the camp chef and her acolytes arose and discovered the altar. For some reason, they didn't think it was funny at all. Was it because they were all women? Or was it because they hadn't had coffee yet? A minor war of words ensued, in which Paul took the brunt of the blame and faced up to accusations of being an insensitive lout.

Paul decided to have a hanging, a purging. Lynch the plastic terror before anyone else felt traumatised by its gross size and innuendo of sadomasochistic sex. They wrapped a rope around its head and it swung from a tree for the rest of their stay in Agua Caliente (that's "hot water" in Spanish).

When it was time to pack up and head north, the group

couldn't just leave the thing there for other campers to ponder, so Paul cut it down and threw it in the wood bin on the side of the trailer.

Everyone forgot about it until the roadblock. The Mexican police were pulling people over and inspecting vehicles. Things went fine as the officers walked around the van and the trailer that held Paul's tour group.

That is, until one of the officers reached into the wood bin and pulled out the dildo.

He stood in glaring sunlight, holding the 40cm-long (16-inch) wand of love in his hand and asked, "Que es esto?" or "What is this?"

The other officers turned and looked. They laughed uproariously for ten minutes, threw it back in the wood bin and waved Paul and his tour forward. They didn't really want an answer.

The next morning, as the chef got out everything for coffee, guess what was on ice? Mr Pink himself. Someone in the group with a sense of humour had decided it was an organ transplant and needed to be preserved—especially since it had saved them at the roadblock, which often requires a bit of bribing to pass through.

It resided in the ice chest next to the eggs and milk until the group reached the border. Because it had been so popular with the gang of Mexican police, Paul decided to show it to the customs officials.

Unfortunately, his Spanish was at the halting, present tense stage. He whipped the dildo out of the ice chest and said, "This is a lethal weapon. Ha ha."

"Weapon?" the officials asked suspiciously.

A few hours of explaining later (still in broken Spanish), Paul and his friends were back on the road. This time, the dildo was thrown in the trailer. People were getting tired of it. The novelty was wearing off. The group, who had been touring for two weeks, wanted to get home and get out of the van.

Weeks went by for Paul, with business as usual, including more trips for his adventure company.

The new secretary back in northern California didn't like the way the office was decorated, so she decided to rearrange things a little. Clean the place up, get rid of the piles of magazines and catalogues cluttering the floor. First, she needed a place to put it all out of sight. The closet.

She saw the dildo.

No one knew how it got in the closet.

She screamed and tossed it—heaved it—over the fence into the neighbour's yard. But it didn't make it over the fence. It got stuck in a tree limb above the office entrance—a definite eye-catcher.

It had to come down, but no matter how hard she shook the tree, it was lodged there. Finally, she called Wencil, who brought over a construction ladder and the dildo went back into the closet.

It disappeared a month ago when Paul wanted to show me the star of this story. I had come to his office to pick up gear for a river trip. He was miffed. Where did it go?

Last week I asked about it again. Paul dug around in the closet. He gave a grunt of surprise—there it was, back on the shelf beside the office supplies.

I jumped back, mouth hanging open, intimidated by the size of the monster dildo from Mexico that just won't go away.

Tales of a Tall Traveller

*David Potts (190cm) from Surfers Paradise,
Queensland. A very tall and very well-liked travel
writer.*

Tall people are not meant to travel. After many years carting my 190cm (6'4") frame around the world and enduring conditions designed to accommodate someone of a more moderate size I've resigned to being a misfit.

Take aircraft for starters. If I'm unlucky enough to be in, um, cattle class, I can guarantee by journey's end my knees will have been concertina-ed into my backbone, especially if the passenger in front opts for a snooze and drops his seat back. At least I don't have a problem reaching into the overhead lockers.

However aircraft seats are not my only problem. Asian coaches tend to be fitted out for the smaller frames of Asian people. On a recent trip I tested every seat to try to find one that provided a more comfortable ride. Only the guide's seat—and no doubt the driver's seat—at the very front of the coach gave my knees any clearance.

Speaking of buses, many years ago, the New South Wales Department of Transport introduced a system of licensing tall passengers to stand on the back platform of their double-decker buses. Anyone over 180cm tall (six feet) and standing in the lower deck would be bent double.

So I turned up to the department's office to be measured for a bus. An official stuck me against a wall, marked the spot with his thumb and declared that I qualified. I was given pass number 164 (which shows not many people knew about the concession or took advantage of it). I flashed it on many occasions when other passengers had to pack the lower deck. I ignored their glares.

Then there are beds. A single bed is a no-no and the biggest no-no of all are bunks in older cruise ships. Usually the bunks were constructed cabin wall-to-cabin wall, and I finish up having to sleep in the foetal position. Sometimes—and only sometimes—I'm lucky enough to find a bunk which does not end in a wall and I can dangle my legs over the end. Most modern cruise ships are much better but even then I sometimes find my feet dangling.

Toilets are another problem. Remember the peculiarly Parisian street loos? The ones built like circular steel port-a-loos, with open roofs, and which sat permanently on sidewalks? I could chat with my spouse—and any other passer-by—over the top while doing my thing.

Some time ago, in a small Japanese village called Moto-Hakone, a brand new public toilet was built out of bricks and glass. It was a very modern design and the locals were probably very proud of it.

The trouble? The bricks may have stopped at a height appropriate for a typical, shorter Japanese male user, but for me, it came up to about my knees. From there it was see-through glass all the way up. When I wanted to relieve myself it was for the whole town to watch, point and giggle...which they did.

Being tall does have one or two advantages. The first is that usually I'm nominated—because I'm identifiable (especially in Asia)—as the rallying point of a tour group and my wife never fears getting lost in a crowd when I'm travelling with her. Instead, she just asks, "Which way the tall fella went?"

The second advantage is that I can usually get a better view of a tourist spot over the heads of my fellow travellers.

Hence, whichever tour operator eventually puts together

a Total Tour for Today's Tall Types will get my vote and probably my tourist dollar!

> *"Like all great travellers, I have seen more than I remember, and remember more than I have seen."*
> —Benjamin Disraeli, 19th century British prime minister

Exploring Mid-winter Vienna in Shorts and a T-shirt
Travel writer Peter Needham, Sydney

The unseemly haste of my last-minute packing had caused me foolishly to pack all my warm winter clothing in my suitcase and check it through to London Heathrow.

As we approached Austria and the pilot mentioned that the country was in the grip of a deep, avalanche-inducing freeze, I realised that my attire (shorts and a T-shirt) would not be suitable.

Vienna was -9°C (or about 16°F) and it was not possible to retrieve clothing from my bag in the hold.

This left a three-choice challenge. I could: (a) spend my precious Austrian half-day stopover sitting at Vienna International Airport; (b) buy warm clothing at the airport and set out to see the sights; or (c) set off into Vienna dressed as I was.

A quick check of the Vienna airport shops gave two warm-clothing alternatives—a leather jacket costing over $2000 when converted into dollars and a duffel coat with horn buttons costing nearly $1000.

I skipped both purchases. Vienna International Airport is connected directly to the city by rail so I decided to make a dash for the city-bound train dressed as I was. The station was chilly—a blizzard blew flurries of snow along the platform and spear-like icicles dangled from the railway signs—but a desperate sprint got me to the train compartment.

It proved to be warm and comfortable, particularly if you hugged the heater.

A pleasant journey through picturesque snow-scapes (complete with hares leaping through the snowdrifts) brought me to Vienna-Mitte station.

Most Viennese, I noticed, were clad in heavy fur coats, large boots and woollen hats.

Moving quickly to avoid death from hypothermia, I found a bar and ordered a Stroh 80, one of the strongest varieties of rum commercially available in Austria. (The 80 indicates it is 80 per cent alcohol.) A few shots of Stroh later, I left the bar exuding a Zen-like inner warmth that defied the frigid conditions, though the barman looked at me strangely.

I bought a hot dog with mustard from a kiosk on Zollamtsstrasse and headed north on foot, T-shirt flapping. My first feeling of alarm came when I saw an enormous white rabbit dart out of a doorway and run across the road. Closer inspection revealed it was somebody dressed in a rabbit outfit.

Not long afterwards, a cat-woman carrying a pitchfork and a man dressed as an apple came bounding towards me along the icy footpath, arm in arm, their breath coming in steamy plumes.

Hallucinations! Phantoms conjured up by cold and schnapps—that must be it! Warm clothing was vital. I had to buy some fast. Running back to Vienna-Mitte train station, shivering by now, I found a department store in the throes of a winter sale. For the equivalent of just $80, I bought an enormous bright yellow vinyl jacket of the sort railway workmen wear when fixing the lines. I also bought a cut-price ski hat that came halfway down my back.

In this super-warm kit, I explored Vienna with ease, returning on the train in time to catch my flight through to London. Once I had settled in London, a little research informed me that my "hallucinations" were actually just participants in the Austrian winter carnival of Fasching, which involves fancy dress.

This little ditty was sent to me by Dick Turner (his real name) who heard it from a friend who heard it from a friend...

I have been in many places, but I've never been in Cahoots. Apparently, you can't go alone. You have to be in Cahoots with someone.

I've also never been in Cognito. I hear no one recognises you there. I have, however, been in Sane. They don't have an airport; you have to be driven there. I have made several trips there, thanks to my friends, family and work.

I would like to go to Conclusions, but you have to jump, and I'm not too much on physical activity anymore.

I have also been in Doubt. That is a sad place to go, and I try not to visit there too often.

I've been in Flexible, but only when it was very important to stand firm.

Sometimes I'm in Capable, and I go there more often as I'm getting older.

One of my favourite places of all to be is in Suspense! It really gets the adrenaline flowing and pumps up the old heart! At my age I need all the stimuli I can get!

I may have been in Continent, and I don't remember what country I was in. It's an age thing.

People Live Here, Right?! Who in Their Right Mind Would have Named This Place?

I've been all over North America, leading tours or writing the tour guides for those tour directors who would follow in my tyre-tracks with paying (and hopefully heavily tipping) passengers in tow.
And I'm always asked by tour leaders if I could please provide some comic relief on the long days of driving. So to keep everyone happy and on the gravy-train track to good tips, I've invented lists of place names that a tour director can deliver in-between toilet stops, with the intention of keeping clients entertained instead of going into comas on the coach. I've attached a short-list for you, in the hope that you might at some stage be able to add to it.
No kidding. These places do really exist and people do live in them:

Badwater, Hog Wallow, Smelley Dog Town, Motley, Tattlersville, Cluttsville, Hurtsboro, The Bottle, Possum Trot, Slick Lizzard, Smut Eye, Dead Horse, Weiner, Blue Balls, Fannie, Hooker, Stinking Bay, Hambone, Climax, Last Chance, Lay, No Name, Yellow Snow, Fluffy Landing, Needmore, Big Beaver Lick, Reddick, Sapp, Two Egg, Wacahoota, BraSwell, Box Springs, Climax, Cumming, Butts, Jinks, Meansville, Snap Finger, Papa, Roachtown, Fickle, What Cheer, Skiddy, Bee Lick, Black Bottom,

Breeding, Grannie, Monkey's Eyebrow, Oddville, Rabbit Hash, Shoulderblade, Klotzville, Hell, Mashpee, Accident, Boring, Scaggsville, Kickapoo, Junior, Plain Dealing, Cummaquid, Dinkytown, Embarrass, Sleepy Eye, Chunky, Chickenbone, Hot Coffee, Improve, Screwdriver, Sweatman, Tightwad, Weed.

And don't forget Truth Or Consequences...

13. DOING IT IN GROUPS

I think I learned before I could even walk, that travel with others was a whole lot better than being some place by myself.

Stand and Deliver!
Fred Walker, North Dakota

The 4.30am wake-up call arrived in the dark of night. It was my idea, so I had no one to blame but myself. Life as a tour guide is not always filled with glamour.

But today started out promising—the group of Australian travel writers was ready for the journey.

I'd set the stage the night before, saying we would watch the sunrise from a place not many people ever had a chance to explore. We were headed into a pristine North Dakota park, where only the weary traveller, the quiet photographer or the hundreds of wild animals roaming the park ventured.

Autumn is a wonderful time to experience the American west. Crowds have thinned, animals are active and the colours range the spectrum from magnificent to spectacular.

But it can also be more than cool at that time of year. The crisp air for a local cuts through a warm-weather guest like a broken glass through butter.

The lesson being learned that day was that no matter how grand your plans, Mother Nature is still in charge! What I had planned for my guests was a morning of wildlife, beautiful scenery and unique experiences, but definitely not the bitter cold wind that nearly drove us off the butte and an unusual no-show of animals that had ensued.

Finally a member of the group asked the unspoken question that was running through all of our minds.

"Will we see a buffalo?"

I was also starting to regret the 4.30am wake-up call. I too was wondering if, "Will we actually see the largest animal in the area that usually are so numerous you have to stop the car and wait for their traffic jams?"

But I kept the shroud of confidence solid and said, "Absolutely, you never know when you may round a corner and run into a handsome herd!"

As the sentence was being spilled from my clenched jaws, we rounded the blind corner and nearly ran into the herd. The squeals of excitement from the back of the van were only overshadowed by the sighs of relief emanating from the guide. Me!

We spent the next 45 minutes hopping in and out of the van, snapping photos from behind the safety and security of the our transport, only to have the rest of the herd join us from the rear and nearly take my scribes along for the ride.

The next 10km (6 miles) out of the park was so loaded with buffalo, the American bison, that by the end of the trip coffee was more on our minds than "Will we actually see a buffalo?" And the coffee I knew was waiting for us at our destination!!

Follow-the-Loud-Mouthed Leader?
Trevor Lake, Sydney

In 1980 I was leading a group into Tibet. The trip was astounding, but we were cursed with a loud-mouthed Chinese guide who was so full of himself that after two days I was determined to put him in his place.

That day we were visiting the Potala Palace. Now, the entrance to the palace is from the back, where one has to climb a steep flight of stairs (some 100 metres) which leads to the roof. From there you descend through the palace to ground level.

As we stood at the base of the steps, the guide was off again about how the stairs were no challenge for him because he was fit and young—but we should take the climb slowly and stop frequently, most especially because any effort at such high altitudes left even the fittest man breathless.

I challenged him to a race to the top of the stairs.

The guide seemed taken aback and said, "I am acclimatised to this altitude and 20 years younger."

"No problem," I announced. "When I was younger I was the 400-metre sprint champion of Australia. In fact, I'll even give you a three-metre start."

This was a challenge his manhood would not allow him to refuse. As we crouched in our starting positions, one of the group screamed, "GO!"

He was off like a rocket. He was determined not just to beat me, but to crush me. He kept the pace up until he was halfway, when he visibly slowed down and his breathing became laboured.

Soon he was down to a jog...the last few metres he dragged his feet one after the other.

But he *was* the first man to the top. He turned around with as big a grin on his face as his agony would allow, only to see me still standing on the bottom step.

"You won!" I shouted.

> "Twenty years from now you will be more disappointed by the things you didn't do than by the ones you did do. So throw off the bowlines, sail away from the safe harbour. Catch the trade winds in your sails. Explore. Dream. Discover."
> —Mark Twain, US author and humourist

Floating Turds and Sailing Nerds
Patricia Sheehan

This is a totally true story. I have been very fortunate to be friends with the same group of women since childhood. Although we don't live in the same states anymore, we still hold reunions once or twice a year, and it feels just like high school.

Since I grew up in New York, and we are all about the same age as the characters in the famous TV series, we are constantly asked, "Which *Sex and the City* girl are you?"

I know I am Carrie Bradshaw. I enjoy writing, I would sell my kidney for the new Prada line and am always in search of a man with a graduate degree, a FICA (US credit) score over 750 and who would love to help me work out Daddy Issues, like Mr Big.

My one friend, who I will refer to as "Maura", can never seem to figure out which *SATC* persona she is.

Here are two universal truths. Daffodils always look better when planted en masse, and if you are a woman with more than three close friends and you don't think you have a slutty friend, well, I have to inform you that you are in fact the slutty friend.

To celebrate my 45th birthday earlier this year, my friends and I decided to put together a last minute Mexican cruise. I flew to Tampa in Florida a day early and stayed at Maura's place.

She has a new boyfriend who I refer to as BABs, short for Broke Ass Bitch. I think his real name is John, but this fits much better. So, the night before the cruise, we all enjoy a few cocktails, and I spend the night down the hall, where I am lulled to sleep by the sounds of them either doing heavy construction or having vigorous relations. I foolishly assume they may be a couple. Oh, how wrong I was.

Hooking up

The next day, our other friends arrive. We board the ship at 10am and by 2pm we have already lost Maura. THE SHIP IS STILL IN THE PORT, and she has already moved on. Maura is smart, professional, educated and would do anything for anyone. But she doesn't believe in buying her own drinks so we know she is with someone who will.

Two days go by and we receive no sign of Maura. We have checked her room, scouted all the bars and now Trish and I are pretty annoyed. We commiserate over several overpriced mixed drinks and have morphed from relaxed cruisers to a professional forensics team.

After hours of investigation, it's 2am and we have to accept defeat. We head up the main staircase when Maura appears. And as a registered nurse, I feel qualified to say she is clearly chemically impaired.

We immediately demand explanations, and it's an interrogation that rivals a John Grisham novel.

Maura begins stammering about a new "friend", an ex (?) Jesuit Priest, and claims that they were at the Build a Bear Workshop. (Do the Build a Bear people serve alcohol?)

For those of you that don't know about Build a Bear, it's a place you take spoiled pre-teens to make their own $100+ stuffed animal, which your dog will either hump mercilessly or destroy moments upon your arrival home. (Mine are humpers.)

So, now, in frustration, I demand to see the bear. I think you already know. There was no bear.

Maura was adamant that she had been in her cabin the past few nights with noise-cancelling headphones and the volume on the house phone turned off.

Yeah, sure.

She then chose to make her exit and sashayed off into a direction not remotely located near her cabin.

To this day, she is as close to me as a sister but I accept that some mysteries will never be revealed. Who built Stonehenge? What is at the centre of a black hole? Where is Jimmy Hoffa buried? Why doesn't Maura have a bear to show for 48 hours in the workshop?

And how high is your blood alcohol level when you seriously think your friends will buy the stuffed animal excuse?

14. MESSING WITH MOTHER NATURE

*"Two roads diverged in a wood and I...
I took the one less travelled by"*
—Robert Frost, US poet

Bear Essentials!

Three British bank tellers pulled me aside the night before our departure on a Trek America Tour to the best national parks of the US and Canadian Rockies.

They'd done their homework, sized up the rest of the Trek and wanted to "parlay" a deal.

They had that wonderful dry humour of the British, and it was clear they'd given the proposal a great deal of consideration while they were pondering the Trek in their local pub back home in Lincolnshire.

The plan was to bribe me, as the Trek Leader, to advise the other nine Trekkers—all females—that we would no doubt be encountering bears while on our adventure, and that it was advised in the guide book to have a man in one's tent for protection.

Playing along with the prank, I did my bear warning at every briefing. Even when we camped on the Circus-Circus casino site in Las Vegas I delivered a straight-faced bear warning with good humour.

Naturally none of the girls were buying any of it... until I rolled into our campsite in Jasper National Park, and there, sitting at our picnic table, was a young bear cub, its mother and another sibling a few metres off, heads buried in a black plastic bag of rubbish.

I've Had a Fair Few Run-ins with Bears

I've got a few thoughts on the animal. I believe that banging pots and pans to ward off bears is a massive misnomer. It just lets them know their dinner is ready.

Even after I delivered a warning to my Trekkers, they ignored me and were visited by a bear.

"I told you before, IF a bear comes into your tent to take your candy bars, you're responsible for all the damage done to your tent..."

This statement rolled off deaf ears, and the two Irish girls who barely escaped the bear went the rest of the trek sleeping under the stars.

No, Not Spare Tyre...Bear Tyre!

In the Black Hills of South Dakota they have a drive-thru Bear Country attraction which, if you believe the epidemic interstate billboards, is more popular than Mt Rushmore and the granite faces of the presidents.

You drive up to the admission window and they charge at you like beat-up-bulls. You get a little map, details of the different bears they've got on the menu and then you roll up your windows, lock your doors and hide the virgins.

Each vehicle then does a drive-by shooting (cameras of course—it's not Los Angeles), passing through monitored electrified gates into the different compounds, driving amid different free-roaming and marauding clusters of bears.

These incarcerated bears work in teams, almost like shop-lifters. The brown bears were the worst. Two approached our Trek van from the front, begging cigarettes and posing as diversions, while the gang leader went around the back, climbed the roof rack ladder, tore through our coolers and off-loaded pickles and packaged potato chips to one of the cubs on the ground. I didn't know bears could climb ladders.

In the next enclosure, an exiled black bear in solitary ate my long-coveted 'Yosemite Sam' tyre cover. I may have avoided the theft if I still had my rear-view mirror intact, but one of the bears in a previous enclosure had borrowed it to apply what I assumed was make-up.

Bank robbers wear balaclavas.

On the way out, I asked if it was possible to regain possession of my car parts. The well-used reply was simply that we'd entered at our own risk.

Blame it on the bears, but I was going to do the rest of the Trek without the use of a rear-view mirror.

The Bear Facts

Did you know that bears can run faster that a horse over short distances?"

I took my tour group to an informative chat about bears in Yosemite National Park one evening. It was delivered by a clever park ranger and, during it, he lightened things up with a little joke.

It was about three guys walking in bear-infested woods, two of them in especially poor shape. One guy says to the others, "Do you know bears can run at up to 80 kilometres (50 miles) an hour?'

And the other replies, "Oh my goodness, if we're attacked we'd never be able to run that fast!"

To which the fellow with running shoes on, the fittest of the three smiles and says, "I don't need to outrun a bear. I only need to outrun you two!"

Bears are Remarkable Climbers and Love Climbing Trees"

I was issued a $200 fine once in the Yosemite Valley for having attracted bears to our camping site. The Bear Warning pamphlet advised us to: suspend any coolers or food chests in the trees, out of the bears' easy reach; avoid having food of any kind in your tents; and most of all, don't even think about leaving honey out to lure in a perfect photo opportunity.

The pamphlet was written for idiots. I strung our coolers by way of a long nylon line over a big branch and anchored it to the heavy picnic table nearby.

It was like flying a red flag to a bull, or projecting vocalisations of a lion on a fresh kill to attract spotted hyena. We might as well have rung a dinner bell.

Bears came in from all quarters, and it took them about two minutes of sizing up the situation to see what needed to be done.

One bear simply moved the picnic table closer under the dinner menu as the others waited patiently. They had seen it all before. As the table got closer to their suspended supper, the cooler got closer to the ground. When they were happy with the access, another bear well trained in opening the cooler latches, stepped up and deftly opened the chest. Dinner spewed forth.

When I told this to the ticket-writing Park Ranger, he said I should have banged a pot with a spoon.

I replied, "Yeah, right, as if having four of them to dinner wasn't enough...I needed to let the others know dinner's on!"

Mountains Topple
Dylan Thomas Sheehan

It was a Sunday, if I recall correctly, in Lake Tahoe, the home of great snow and small taxes and where California and Nevada meet.

I had woken up with a cup of coffee for energy and

several pieces of ham for protein and sustenance, along with the American special of half-and-half cereal to sugar ratio. Everything the body needs for another day snowboarding on the mountain.

This particular day was not just any day but the last day, roughly translating to the most important day. It comes down to those last hours. It will be what you'll dream about months after the season is gone.

I'll tell you one thing. I sure as hell was going to make the most out of that day. So, after breakfast, I suited up with the usual routine, involving several squats while picking up my boots followed by a few extras with the incestuous packing of my bags.

As due course dictates we were in the car by 9am. I was accompanied by my family, which included one sister (Hayley), one brother (Cody), one mother (Bridget) and one father (Mark). Also there were the Bouskilla family, who were travelling in their own car.

The day moved on accordingly, with little to no divisions for normality. Remi Bouskilla and I, being longtime friends, rode together as the others teamed up with their own partners.

Several hours into the trip, and only a few left of the day. Remi and I rode in single file. Me following behind him and closely hitting the same spots.

It was a run we had done a few times before that day and it made a story out of an otherwise normal ride. Remi, leading the way, jumps onto a box which didn't seem to be much of a threat. I followed and with smooth precision jumped onto the box. Impressed with my own style, I contemplated my skills and then I slipped. My chest and side rammed suddenly into the cold sharp corner of the box as my lungs tried to tear threw my chest. I fell hard on the snow, and in an attempt to composed myself stood suddenly and continued riding.

Halfway down I turned to Remi and stated, "Jesus, mate. I just got the shit kicked out of me by the box!"

He replied vaguely with, "Yeah? That sucks. Which run do you wanna do next?"

I considered the runs on offer and decided I should check out my injury so I mentioned something about "needing a minute". A minute later I'm in pain so, as anyone in unrecognisably horrible pain does, I headed to the first aid station only to pass out on the way.

Someone had to take me there. When the doctors asked me for a urine sample in one of those little cups, I handed back a small glass of what looked like tomato juice. I was steadily leaking red fluids inside.

When my folks arrived, the attending doctors said they were not set up for what ailed me, so I was carted off to the emergency room of the hospital in Truckee, California, about 18km (11 miles) away.

I'd been in this very same place eleven years earlier to the day, because my kid sister Hayley was born here. And it was her birthday. Ironically, I'd be staying a lot longer than she did. After X-rays and my old man fretting on the phone with the insurance company in Australia, I was planted in the Intensive Care Unit so the doctors could pamper my lacerated spleen and badly bruised kidney. I tossed in a few badly bruised ribs for good measure.

For the next couple weeks I ate nice food, watched about fifty American TV channels and didn't have to do school work or rock up for my after-school job.

All in all, falling off the mountain on the last run, and on the last day of our Lake Tahoe holiday, turned out OK. The nurses were very, very nice too.

Because the flight home would take fourteen hours and I was still sore, we were upgraded...and I always like sitting in the front!

The moral of the story is, if you do have to fall off a mountain, try to make it on the last day of your holiday, not the first! My friend recently sent me a postcard saying he spent about an hour having fun on day one and the rest of the time in bed!

At least I got the timing right! Last day, Last run, Last hour!

15. NATIONAL PARKS

The Grand Canyon—Good Things Are Worth Waiting For!

"When it Rains, It Pours!" was the slogan used by the Morton Salt Company in the US to promote its iodised salt, which didn't clump-up or go soggy when it got damp.

I recall the pen and ink artwork on the container which boasted a little girl in a torrential downpour, under an umbrella with her cylinder of Morton Salt, safe and dry, cradled in her arm.

I loved that image. Maybe if the guys at Morton read this, they'll send me an old poster.

Because the Grand Canyon is on every touring itinerary that passes remotely close to the state of Arizona, it rightfully gets a lot of attention by tourists and touring buses. I've led groups through the region for 20 years and counting, but some highlights about that place simply stick out.

I've had hundreds of passengers at the Grand Canyon, so many I've lost count. However, I have an informative little routine I go through religiously before we arrive there.

It goes something like this...

"OK guys, Listen up! First thing. The Grand Canyon is a BIG mother, 385 miles (620km) around and a mile (1.6km) straight down! And the rim is 7000 feet (2.1km) above sea level.

"This means the air is a lot thinner, so if you feel a wee bit tipsy and tired, it's more than likely you're not used to sucking in the thinner air. You might also get a headache if you overdo things, so tread gently."

"Oh yeah. Go very easy on the booze or you'll be off the launching pad before you finish the first glass of grog. The good nectar goes straight into your system at that altitude and it can easily alter your attitude.

"At this height, you'll soon discover that the burning ultraviolet rays of the sun are 35 per cent more potent than at sea level, so please cover your asses and other body parts up. Wear hats, use sunscreen and avoid the heat of the day. Water can freeze on the rim at 5am and it can get up to 100°F (38°C) at the bottom of the Colorado River by noontime, so drink water!

"I know some of you plan to do the hike down to the Colorado River and back in one day. You'll need to leave camp for the rim no later than 5am, tote your own water, use heaps of sunscreen and carry a flashlight. You'll be walking in the dark for a few hours at either end of the track—and do remember that when you get to the bottom, you're going down the Kaibab Trail and UP the Bright Angel trail. The North Rim trails will take you a few hundred miles away from your shower towels and tents."

This group appeared to be in a coma, so I made them repeat what I'd just said. They reminded me they were "not school children", but I made them do it anyway. I expected no misunderstandings.

My lovely New Zealand virgin was highly excited about hiking the trail during daylight hours and just as excited at letting me have my way with her lower unit after dark. I was also excited, in anticipation of providing a memorable visit to the roof-rack and the meat and greet of her tender loins when she came out of the canyon that evening.

I was going to yodel in a New Zealand canyon while visiting the Grand Canyon, bridging two monumental international attractions. I'd already purchased shower tokens and towels for us at the Bright Angel Lodge.

See, they charge for water at the Grand Canyon because they have to truck the stuff in from Williams, Arizona, so a shower cost five dollars for six minutes.

Everything looked wonderful, except for the part when everything went pear-shaped.

The three British bank blockheads had openly ignored my warnings to cover up with sunblock.

England hadn't seen the sun for a few hundred years, so this trio elected to burn to the crimson red of a crock-cooked lobster. It was the first occasion where I noticed that skin could actively bubble.

I dutifully delivered all three of the jelly-shouldered idiots to the emergency room, and accomplished this trip at the same time I was delivering the German gal who'd gotten light-headed and fallen at the ice cream stand. She broke her wrist in two places and did a head-plant into a double-decker chocolate cone. With chocolate sprinkles. I only know this because her other light-headed tent-mate took a picture.

This left me just enough time to swing by the Ranger Station and collect the three rowdy wrestling Australians, whose sea-level intake of alcohol at 7000 feet landed them in the lock-up with the local law. Even though they were only joking, the Park Police suggested it is not at all funny to attempt throwing your mates off the rim of the canyon. Remember boys, it is a mile straight down after all.

After evaluation and observation, I was able to assure the Park Police and a very cute female Park Ranger that none of these blokes was likely to lob themselves off anything higher than the rim of the toilet bowl. I was granted permission to take them home and put them straight into their tents.

The pretty Park lass (I'm a sucker for a gal in a uniform) offered to accompany me, but knowing that I had my lovely Virgin New Zealander on the menu, I gallantly declined her help. We'd meet up again within hours.

My "date" for the evening still hadn't showed up for showering, deflowering and towelling off, so I went back to the campsite thinking perhaps I'd missed her with all my other comings and goings.

And there, sitting at the Trek site, was the pretty Park Ranger. She had a note from the North Rim Ranger Station radio dispatcher which stated they had a girl up there who'd taken the wrong trail and hiked up the other side of the Grand Canyon. The Rangers on that side of the Canyon said "they'd be keeping her and taking good care of her overnight."

The following day, I high-tailed in by road to the North Rim to collect my prize, which had already been plucked by a Park Ranger from Minnesota with chiselled good looks and a starched uniform.

The mid-westerner had taken the job to get away from the Minnesota mosquitoes which some claimed, also doubled as the state's bird.

And he got my bird, The Bastard.

Skunks, Possums, Porcupines and Pickled Persons

The campground in White's City, New Mexico, although dusty and often filled with mad bikers on Harley-Davidsons bent on never sleeping, was one of my favourites. The sunsets were always magnificent, and from the butte where Trekkers pitched their tents you could see seemingly forever to the horizon.

The toilets were very clean, and the showers we threw four quarters at to enjoy were perched over a panoramic view of the Guadalupe Mountains. They had floorboards for you to tread instead of concrete, and I always appreciate the little extras when showering...

The big attraction to being at the doorstep of Carlsbad Caverns was the bats parade each evening, when millions of bats swarmed out of the caves to feed.

The downside to the campground was that it was in the middle of nowhere, with no petrol, no shopping to speak of and heaps and heaps of nocturnal visitors.

The wind could also tear through the area with hurricane force and send a convoy of camp tents bouncing off into the distance like tumbleweeds.

A road sign for the campground threatened, "The Neighbours Are Noisy!" and depicted all manner of wildlife in store for anyone brave enough to drop in overnight.

The owners did it as advertising, but they should have really offered the noisy news as a warning. After all, cigarette manufacturers have to now state, on every packet, that the contents may kill you.

16. MONEY MAKES THE WORLD GO ROUND

"When preparing to travel, lay out all your clothes and all your money. Then take half the clothes and twice the money"
—Anon

Don't Leave Home Without It!
Louie, whilst cleaning his .357 Magnum

In 1967, I lied to my mother when I told her we were going to Florida under the protection of Louie's dad. My good buddy Louie Purchase got a six-pack of cheap tickets to Miami on a plane his dad was flying.

We, naturally, had fake ID and no place to stay. I recall looking out the window of the plane at 30,000 feet (9140 metres), thinking about how the entire world was covered in snow. Louie pointed out the fact that I was an idiot. I was looking down onto the cloud cover with sun shining on it.

Fort Lauderdale was fabulous. We slept under a bridge on the inter-coastal waterway a fair few nights, or snuck into the rooms of friends after their parents had drifted off to after-cocktail comas.

Our fake proof didn't work in most places, but greedy small-shop owners seemed willing to sell us beer by the case, as long as we said we'd drink it in someone else's neighbourhood.

That trip was a real eye-opener for me. I'd had my new sports coat stolen at the airport, been burned to a crisp by the Florida sun, shot down by numerous girls from good families, and still I was addicted to the idea of travel. No plan, no money and an open page to fill...

"A journey is like marriage. The certain way to be wrong is to think you control it."
—John Steinbeck, US author

The One-armed Bandit We Call the ATM!

Whilst tapping my watch to make a point, I told the assembled coach load of overseas visitors that our tour would be leaving Los Angeles for the glittering lights of Las Vegas in fifteen minutes.

Their luggage was already loaded, and they could grab a cuppa or settle up their extras with the hotel reception and we were going to light-out-on the dot.

On day one of any tour, it's important to get everyone on the same page.

One of my Australian passengers had already made himself well known to me because of his dissatisfaction with the view from his room, his request for a historical detailing of the San Andreas Fault—and a complaint from my coach driver, who said the fellow had just purchased a lawnmower in a heavy brown box that he expected to have placed in the safety of his hotel room each night of a 21-day tour.

While my other excited travellers were eagerly lining up for good seats on the bus, our awkward Australian grumbled his way to the ATM machine in the lobby, placed his newly acquired debit card in the slot and proceeded to take a guess at his new password.

After three failed attempts, the machine does what they all do nowadays. It ate his card and advised him to contact his bank if he dreamed of getting it back.

I only know this because hotel security brought the fact he was kicking the machine and screaming bloody murder to my attention when they called the El Segundo cops.

I arrived on the scene just as they were about to taser the Tasmanian terrorist.

He had over $25,000 of his own money in that account,

he shouted, and the "f***ing infernal machine" refused to cough up a plug penny.

And he insisted that the entire group wait for him until it did. In fact, I was personally summoned to not move a single muscle. So I did what any professional tour director would have done, and called the office to say I wanted to get rid of this asshole ASAP if not sooner.

The office was non-committal on leaving him behind. I agreed to delay our departure by an hour, to see if he could sort himself out. Otherwise, I'd be, most regrettably, forced to leave him behind and he'd have to simply catch up with us in Las Vegas.

His reply was very verbal. Threats were tossed at me from across the hotel lobby like projectiles.

An hour and three minutes later, our driver, sporting nothing short of admiration for me, removed the lawnmower and two other suitcases from the belly of our German-engineered whale.

We waved to the chap as he stood at the curb side, arms crossed and threatening enormous legal action. He would have my job and my company would rue the day. "Hoorays" echoed loudly from the other 49 passengers as we pulled away and the bloke never did rejoin the tour.

He later lodged a colossal claim against the company, and was awarded a partial refund of the tour price by the court. My group supported my decision to leave him in our dust and contributed heavily to my tips at the tour's end.

We got off to a bad start, and I sometimes feel for the fella when I go to the ATM and inject my plastic.

I've committed my PIN numbers to heart. Although I sometimes forget what I've had for breakfast (like now) and my birthday, I never, ever forget that PIN.

17. SAY CHEESE!

Everyone has a photographic memory. Some just don't have film...

Shutter Speed! African Snapshot—the Road Kill Was Almost Me

I was in Tsavo National Park in Kenya, and noted four fresh kills along the roadside with only a few bites of fresh flesh torn from the hindquarter of each one.

There was no sign of a lion or hyena anywhere, just the oddly dropped wildlife. Not even the carcass-oriented vultures had arrived for lunch.

I took pictures of each kill, hoping to get some answers from the animal gurus at the next stop. I used the photo-taking to also diffuse the in-car fight I'd just had with my female travelling companion. The chance to step away from the car, even for a few moments, afforded me a few wisps of emotional blue sky.

When I got back into the vehicle, I'd be reminded again that the brochures warned against leaving one's car. This nagging notion only fuelled my fire to flee.

When I spotted a zebra kill about 20 metres off the track with the same markings—only a small bite torn from the hindquarters—I stopped, reloaded the idiot camera and prepared to walk into the scrub for a closer shot. My lass, again, issued serious warnings about leaving the safety of the car, tapping the brochure with her forefingers. And again, I ignored her.

The moment the shutter clicked, I saw the two ears of a lounging lioness perk up to her next meal on an adjoining ant mound. She had been sleeping and was so well camouflaged I'd not seen her.

Everything happened faster than the autodrive on the camera after the click of the shutter. I ran the 50-metre dash in 5.9 seconds in high school, not nearly fast enough to get me from a standing start and back to the car safely, but my choices were slim and very far between. So I threw the lioness the camera and took to my heels.

I could hear my car mate screaming. When I reached the car I dove straight over the hood, contorted and dove through an open back window. My heart was pounding, my companion was simultaneously hugging me and hitting me in turn...and the lioness? Well, she just took pictures.

She'd been distracted from eating me by the camera and every time a paw hit the camera just right the autodrive would advance to the next frame.

She shot an entire roll of film that day, and when I finally came to some semblance of composure, I nudged the car into the bush.

I honked my horn, revved the motor and shouted obscenities to the lion until she batted my camera into the scrub and moved on. When I retrieved it, it was sandy and slobbered on, but for the most part still very much intact.

My car mate showed me the part of the Tsavo visitors' guide that said there was a 20,000 shilling (about $250) fine for leaving your vehicle in an undesignated area, if convicted. I asked if the fine applied if I'd been eaten off-road.

Most surprising were the pictures I got from the reclaimed camera. The lioness had taken some pretty good photos–one of which was a blurred image of me high-tailing it for the car's bonnet.

"Proper Planning Prevents Poor Performance"
Mark Sheehan, Florida Keys

The Florida Keys featured some type of Holiday Inn hotel

on most of the bigger atolls, and we would be bunking for free at every place that had rooms. It was, all of it, going to be "on the house".

The Holiday Inn in Key Largo boasted the original boat used in the filming of *The African Queen*; the unforgettable 1951 film with Humphrey Bogart and Katharine Hepburn. The worm-rotted hull was tied up at the dock outside the hotel to lure nurses from Nisswa, Minnesota to the nearby pool bar.

By the time we met the nurses, all three of us were sporting some caramel-coloured skin tones. The girls, fresh off the plane from Minnesota, were as white as snow-covered cattle.

They openly engaged us at the poolside and collectively wrote postcards to their milk-white boyfriends back home. Shane took photos, Jack wrote strong and silent journal entries and I created engaging conversation before retreating in search of a cold glass of milk.

By the time I returned, the sun was dropping. Inhibitions had also taken a nosedive with the introduction of the poolside Happy Hour.

Even the leather-barked bartender appeared well lubricated, drawing double shots all around and doing a fair few of them himself. The waitress, who knew him from kindergarten, suggested he not operate any farm equipment at closing time.

Wanna See the Tattoo of My Mouse?

I knew the entire team had loosened up a lot in my absence when a local gal in cut-off shorts asked if we'd like to see her new tattoo of a MOUSE.

Sure, we chirped, why not? The bartender had just

shown us an anchor on his left shoulder.

The lit-up lass unzipped her shorts and pulled what could hardly be called clothing down around her kneecaps, to show the entire assembly what the Minnesota girls claimed was a "perfectly shaved beaver".

The gal's punch line was a real attention getter (as if we weren't already riveted to the view) when she exclaimed in a surprised southern accent... "Oh my goodness, my PUSSY must have eaten it!"

It all went downhill from there. Naturally we all tipped heavily.

No Point Crying Over Spilt Milk

My love of well-chilled milk is no secret and I'll travel many miles to find it.

I often say I could give up beer in bottles before handing over the good oil from the tits of heifers. But it's got to be gulped cold and now, as I've matured and my bones are brittle, I prefer low-fat, low calcium, (2%). I can drink a few litres a day with ease, but it has got to be as cold as a well-digger's ass.

Every good road trip develops a rhythm of its own, so when the sun dropped we enlightened the Minnesota misses as to where the good watering holes were. We then sauntered off to our free and adjoining rooms to shower, shave and make preparations for a night at the Mad Monkey Saloon, appropriately named after the owner. They boasted a live local band every evening.

Back in my free room, I noted my milk had lost its crisp, cool edge. So I ran the cold water into the sink, letting my milk jug swim while I showered.

When I'd finished, the milk was still not cold enough to guzzle, so I increased the pressure, added some of the hotel's free ice to the sink and settled down on my bed for a catnap.

I woke up to Shane pounding on my door. He had just taken a distress call from the hotel's night manager, saying the family below me was in need of a lifeboat. Water was pouring through the light fixtures at an alarming rate.

I stepped out of bed to find my flip-flops floating past. Mind you, the milk was cold.

Costly Communications
—The Qantas Cover-Up!

"A big painted bird took away my old man..."
—Joni Mitchell, US singer

Jane Corbett-Jones was the brilliant public relations guru of Ansett Airlines in Australia for years, and she had the media pleasantly wrapped around her fine fingertips. Jane knew Everybody who was Anybody.

So when the airline launched its first international flight plans and delivered a spanking new Boeing 747 to Sydney, Jane was going to pull out all the stops for the Ansett Airlines Event of the Year. She attracted travel writers, the press, TV and radio icons like moths to an outback flood light.

Celebrities were salted through the crowd, boasting business class boarding passes on the house, and there was even a red carpet rolled out on the tarmac, for the media to board the plane and view the insides of the sleek flying machine after the official ribbon-cutting speeches.

A famous chef created the on-board menu and glorious food was laid on, the plane was spit-polished and positioned where it had a brilliant backdrop.

All was in place to capture headlines for weeks afterwards. Champagne, good cheer and great food flowed freely.

Jane had lured over 300 media moguls to the event, and as she stepped up to welcome everyone a tractor rounded the corner of the Qantas hangers, towing a new Boeing 747 with the entire aircraft covered in Aboriginal artwork from bow to stern.

The driver towed in dangerously close to the Ansett event's bird, and the entire media group that Jane had worked months to assemble ran off to grab the first shots of the enemy tail-feathers. Qantas had stolen the show, and Jane had paid for the sandwiches.

For months afterwards Qantas made front covers across the country, and the globe, with stories a-plenty being submitted by the very folks

Jane had seduced to create coverage for her brand. Ouch, that had ta hurt!

Overweight Luggage
If bags can do it, why can't I?

Submitted by our wonderful son Cody William Sheehan. All our kids love to travel!

About a year or so ago, like many young Aussies do, I decided to venture off to the land of my ancestors in the UK and Europe. I was hunting for new sights, insight and above all downright fun!

I went with a totally cool tour group known as Contiki,

which is a collection of 18 to 35-year-olds intent on seeing the world while still in "party" mode. It was the bus that offered up the best of both worlds: the sightseeing and, of course, the playful partying!

I was on my second leg of the tour, called European Spirit, which started in Paris and went down to Rome via Amsterdam, Croatia and the Czech Republic.

We had stopped in the beautiful city of Florence (or Firenze, as the Italians call it—we did have a tour guide on board!) for one night only to act like the stars: sunset photos, everyone all dolled up in shirts, dresses, and heels. And that was just the guys! We were all out on the town, and our guide said dress like we owned the place.

Our first stop was the statue of Michelangelo and then off to dinner for a special meal created just for our group. After dinner we went to a small local club to celebrate two on-board birthdays.

Things were starting to quieten around midnight so I went back with the earlier group on the bus.

Once everyone was on board, the REAL party started. The music was cranking on high with all the best hit tracks and the aisle was filled with people dancing and moving about any way that the many chairs would allow.

After about five minutes of this awesomeness a new-found friend of mine said, "Hey, I reckon Cody could fit up there", pointing to the slender overhead bag rack.

I said, "You really think so?"

He offered encouragement and, right out a Nike commercial, said, "Just Do it."

So with a little help from my friends and the nearby armrests, I hoisted myself up placing my entire 185cm (6'1") of body flat along the bag rack.

I JUST fit! I could feel a slight squeeze around me as the

cradle I was in hugged me.

When everyone saw me up there they started chanting, "Cody in the bag rack, Cody in the bag rack!"

And the revellers carried the tune all the way back to our overnight village.

When our tour manager saw me up there, she said, "That sounds about right! Only on Contiki!"

PERSONAL FUNNY STORIES

PERSONAL FUNNY
STORIES

PERSONAL FUNNY STORIES

PERSONAL FUNNY STORIES

NOTES

NOTES

NOTES

NOTES

ACKNOWLEDGEMENTS

I'm being a lot smarter this time around and not thanking, or exposing anyone by their real name, unless they've willing asked for it in providing the petrol for these pages. Unless contributors have already given me a written thumbs-up and full-throttle-clearance to put the landing gears down, I'm not naming names.

If you do come to find yourself in this book, I'm banking on the notion that you'll still look kindly towards me sleeping on your sofa after reading it. And maybe nobody who knows you, will figure out it's you.

This book would have never, ever gotten off the runway if it weren't for the wonderful people who make up the New Holland Publishing team. Jodi De Vantier, my editor, possesses the patience of numerous saints. Lliane Clarke is my mentor and my Max Perkins, with a wonderful scribe-side manner that has helped me form every book I've written under New Holland's banner. Lesley Pagett is lovely, and a suitable candidate for cloning. Ishbel Thorpe, who runs the front end of the office, has always greeted me with smiles, and put my long-winded calls through even when she shouldn't.

Fiona Schultz, the alpha gal, has consistently seen the good idea, the story worth telling and graciously allowed me the leeway to write books that please me in the doing. I'm spoilt at New Holland Publishers.

Thank You! Thank
You, Thank You!

Everyone has a good travel story to tell and some of my
buddies had a fair few to share. My inbox was overwhelming and
created real challenges to a manuscript that was meant to be petite
enough to fit into your top pocket, and be carried discreetly back and forth to
the toilet on an airplane. Reading it under the covers with a flashlight would not
put too much pressure on the EverReady™ batteries. So what you're holding in your
hands, is only the tip of the pick, mixed in and melded with some of my stuff but I'd like to
thank everyone we asked who stepped up:

Jack Benson, Shane Boocock, Beth Feely, Louie Purchase, Craig Rich, Timmy Meehan,
Tom Kennedy, Betsy Mellons, Danny Haggerty, Richard Branson, Barbi Benton, Andrea Black,
Cody Sheehan, Dylan Sheehan, David Sheehan, James T. Olsen, Anne Olsen, Anne Rheingold,
Hayley Sheehan, Tracy Spicer, Catriona Rountree, Michel Palin, Ruth McCartney, John Cleese,
Tom Travers, Nancy Friedman, Martin Korn, David Laughlin, Randy Fraiser, Tracy Cannata,
Gary Dickson, Gayle Dickson, Cherie Sheehan, Bart Sheehan, Patrick Sheehan, Ellie Sheehan,
Nana Fink, Elisa Elwin, Deb Dixon Smith, Mike Smith, Andy Purvis, Kirby Sandberg, Tony
Church, Jeremy James, Harry Antonio, Tom Williams, Mark Grundy, Tony Baily, Todd
Matea, Maria Toi, John Lockhart, Peter Smith, Trevor Lake, Mike Freed, Randy Freed,
Bill Bryson, John Cruwys, John Cachia, Veronica Matheson, Mike Lillie, Geoffrey
Hutton, Monique Roos, Robert Sheehan, Edward Esteve, Christopher Sheehan,
Chris Petty, Helen Wong, Trent Brewer, Mario Ferro, Hayley Catherine
Sheehan, Steve Avinzino, Norb Vonnegut, Mary Vonnegut, Carson
Scott, Ben Sheehan, Laura Purvis, Kathy Nightingale, Gordon
Swire, Nick Wayland, James Wilkinson, Glenn A.
Baker, Kamahl, Colin Finkelde, Mark
Waters, Paul Adams,

Elizabeth Adams, John
Meakin, Lynsey McCaffrey
(Hurley),Caroline Mankey, Jessie Brain, Geoffrey
Brain, Barbara Stafford, Fred Walker, Marlee Montana,
Connie Peters, Maria Diez, Joe Harding, Chelsea Rozanski, Carol
Goldberg, Leo Hogan, Tim Leaf, Susan Wilson, Penny Church, Amy
Landers,Louise Goldsbury, Sol Walkling, Scott Cammell, Barry Mayo, Bart
Sheehan, Margaret Drobot, Silvio Barretta, Michael Willis, Bridget Sheehan,
Caroline Davidson, Lou Hockel, Nora Saxton, Judith Miller, Lucy Steffens, Lori
Armstrong, Ed Solomon, Jackie Solomon, Jo Solomon, Tatyana Golyanich, Jason Leo,
Diana Plater, Rob McFarland, Jane-Corbitt-Jones, KimDavis, Alison Henderson, Rob
Coulthurst, Chris Esteve, Beth Feely, Rick Bennett, Karen Viehoever, Andrew Lucero,
Simone Mills, Bill Ofgant, Stanley Rand, Cliff Leeds, Chris Barnaby, Mike Gallagher, Doc
Holiday, Jennifer Ackerson, Anne Rheingold, John Walsh, David Rayne, Brian O'Heir, Lisa
Alpine, Harry Yaghlejian, Blaise Winter, Dick Turner, Bill James, Yon Shin Willis, Dallas
Newton, Jack Akkaus, Rusty Bennitt, Hank Hofford, Michael Carmody, Bernard Groseclose,
Charlie Carmody, John Wilson, Ted Turner, Bruce Piper, Lynne Izzo, LaDonna Alfino, Julie
Flowers, Julie Miller, Sally Hammond, Peter Fiske, David Potts, Eric Gibson, Meghan
Singleton, Freed Walker, Tim Richards, Holly Regan, Nina Mori, Barry Matheson, Stuart
Forsaith, Harry Powell, Beth Blakmer, Melissa Brown, Joan Math, Nancy Greiner, Glen
Lehrman, Bob Rickey, Allison Anderson, Kevin Jan, Hannah Anderson, Laura
Powers, Jeff Zack, Paul Campbell, Sarah Dye, Lesley Cooper, Jon Handlery,
Susan Gough Henley, John Savage, John Kerr, Kristie Kellahan, Sam Cox,
Bob Davidoff, Mimi Dossett, Louis Wilcox, Tom Nicholson, Ken
Barsa, Jo Palmer, Chris Macintire, Rod Bennett, Gary
Manuel, Moria McLean, James Gaskell, & Dan
Enoch and Vivienne Westwood.

First published 2012 by
New Holland Publishers Pty Ltd
London • Sydney • Cape Town • Auckland

1/66 Gibbes Street Chatswood NSW 2067 Australia
Garfield House 86–88 Edgware Road London W2 2EA United Kingdom
218 Lake Road Northcote Auckland New Zealand
Wembley Square First Floor Solan Road Gardens Cape Town 8001 South Africa
www.newhollandpublishers.com
www.newholland.com.au

A record of this book is held at the National Library of Australia

ISBN9781742572079

Publisher: Fiona Schultz
Publishing director: Lliane Clarke
Designer: Stephanie Foti
Production director: Olga Dementiev
Printer: McPhersons Printing Group
Front Cover: Kimberley Pearce
Illustration by: Shane Boocock

10 9 8 7 6 5 4 3 2 1

Keep up with New Holland Publishers on Facebook
http://www.facebook.com/NewHollandPublishers